Reading
Public
Libraries

Reference Department

PRINT FOR PARTIAL SIGHT

A report to the Library Association Sub-committee
on Books for Readers with Defective Sight

by

Alison Shaw MA

A research project supported by a grant from the
Viscount Nuffield Auxiliary Fund

London

The Library Association

1969

© The Library Association 1969
S B N 85365 311 9

Text set on the IBM 370 in Press Roman
and printed in Great Britain by
Hobbs the Printers Ltd., Millbrook, Southampton.

Contents

Acknowledgements

A great many people, among them members of the Sub-committee and those in welfare departments, voluntary organisations and schools for the partially-sighted, have helped during the course of the investigations described in this report – I would like to thank them all.

I am particularly grateful to Mr. A.H. Briggs for his encouragement and advice: to Mrs. Joan Kell and Dr. E.C. Poulton for their constructive comments and ideas: and to Mr. David Hill of the Medical Research Council Computer Unit for the help he gave with the statistical design of the tests and the analysis of their results.

But above all I would like to thank all the people – old and young – who, by answering questions and reading print samples, provided the basic data for the study.

A.S.

Members of the Sub-committee on Books for Readers with Defective Sight

J. BEBBINGTON, F.L.A. City Librarian and Information Officer, Sheffield: *Chairman of the Sub-committee, 1963-1964*

A.H. BRIGGS, M.B., Ch.B., D.O.M.S. Ophthalmic Surgeon, County Hospital, Lincoln

MRS. J.M. CLARKE, A.L.A. Hospital Librarian, St. Thomas's Hospital

I.M. DUGUID, M.D., Ph.D., F.R.C.S.: representing Moorfields Eye Hospital

MISS M.J. LEWIS, A.L.A. Lecturer, School of Librarianship, North-Western Polytechnic

W.A. MUNFORD, M.B.E., B.Sc. (Econ.), Ph.D., F.L.A. Librarian and Director-General, National Library for the Blind

MISS J.M. PLAISTER, B.Sc. (Econ.), F.L.A. Director, South Eastern Regional Library System

P.W. PLUMB, F.L.A. Senior Lecturer, School of Librarianship, North-Western Polytechnic: *Chairman of the Sub-committee, 1965-1969*

MISS J.M. RHODES, A.L.A. Deputy County Librarian, Dorset

R. STURT, M.A., F.L.A. Head, Department of Administrative Studies, College of Librarianship, Wales

R.F. VOLLANS, F.L.A. Assistant City Librarian, Westminster

P.M. WHITEMAN, F.L.A. Deputy Director, School of Library Studies, Queen's University of Belfast

G.M. WILLIAMS, Headmaster, Brookfield House School, Woodford Green, Essex: representing The National Association for the Education of the Partially Sighted

M. YELLAND, B.A., A.L.A. Research Officer, Library Association: *Secretary to the Sub-committee*

MISS M.H.T. YUILLE, M.A. Librarian, Institute of Ophthalmology

Foreword

by

ARNOLD SORSBY, C.B.E., M.D., F.R.C.S.

Emeritus Professor in Ophthalmology at the Royal College of Surgeons and the Royal Eye Hospital

The first consideration for legibility to those with defective sight is visibility both of the letters themselves and of the features which give them individuality. A large letter which is badly formed or poorly printed may well be less recognisable than a smaller letter void of these defects. But there is more to the act of reading than the recognition of the individual letters. All readers, whether normal or partially-sighted, have to contend with the complex of factors that make for legibility, particularly ease and accuracy of perception of words as distinct from letters. Some of these factors involve mental activity, but others are dependent on such intact ocular functions as saccadic movements and a full field. This tangle of cerebral, oculo-motor and ocular factors _ to say nothing of such environmental factors as adequate illumination and comfort – is not made any the less formidable by the fact that partial-sight has no exact meaning. It clearly excludes both total blindness and normal sight, but this still leaves a very wide range of visual disability. Furthermore the more severe of these various degrees of partial-sight are not necessarily stationary; in fact progressive deterioration is not uncommon particularly in the elderly. The different degrees of partial-sight have therefore qualitative as well as quantitative aspects.

As to the number of partially-sighted, no convincing assessment can be made. It is obviously much more than the 33,545 registered in England and Wales as at 31st December 1967, for it is known that registration as partially-sighted – first initiated in 1948 – is still grossly inadequate. Furthermore a considerable proportion of the 102,597 registered as blind at that date – and this figure too is well below the real incidence – have sight better than 3/60; they are thus close to the partially-sighted and can be grouped with them in the context of the present study. Clearly, partial-sight – or partial blindness, to put it more brutally but as accurately – is not an insignificant problem numerically.

For reasons brought out in the present study, no serious attention has been paid until recent years to the difficulties that the partially-sighted have in obtaining printed books that they can see to read. The books that are now being produced by Mr. F.A. Thorpe's Ulverscroft Press have vividly highlighted this neglect, and are in themselves no mean achievement. No less gratifying is the generosity of the Viscount Nuffield Auxiliary Fund in making possible the present study on print suitable for the partially-sighted. Till now mainly subjective judgements have gone into the production of books for the partially-sighted. With Miss Alison Shaw's assessment of the factors in legibility as determined in a series of tests with 288 adults and 48 children with partial-sight, objective data critically collected and as critically analysed are now available. Her findings dispose of some venerable traditions, and have established simple and clear guidance for the selection of type, and for the spacing of letters. A series of further questions – the length of line, the arrangement of type and paper, colour contrasts between print and paper, and the presentation of illustrations – are now all well defined issues that can be pursued in the light of the findings recorded in this admirable study. Further ahead lie exploration of possible modifications of typography in relation both to the reader's eye trouble and his physical capacities.

In initiating this investigation the Library Association has rendered a great potential service to the partially-sighted. It is to be hoped that publishers, printers and the welfare authorities will help to translate this potentiality into a reality. There are many good reasons for doing so and they need not be stressed. But, there is also one very bad but compelling reason, namely that here as in all other efforts that aim at alleviation and relief, it is not only the handicapped who benefit. Today, everywhere, the hale and hearty enjoy advantages that have evolved from facilities created yesterday for the handicapped.

Part I

Background to The Project

1.0 THE LIBRARY ASSOCIATION'S INTEREST

This report is an account of a research project on the design of
reading material for the partially-sighted. Its purpose has been to
collect some reliable facts that would help printers and publishers
to produce more legible books for readers with defective sight. In the
course of analysing these facts a number of points have come to
light that will be of interest not only to printers and publishers, but
also to those concerned in other ways with the education and welfare
of the partially-sighted.

The project has not been concerned with Braille and the problems
of blind readers unable to see even the largest print, but with people
who are able to do some print reading but have difficulty in seeing
normal print easily.

The study was carried out between April 1966 and September 1968,
and was financed by a grant to the Library Association from the
Viscount Nuffield Auxiliary Fund. The work consisted of an objective
investigation into the effect on legibility of variations in design,
weight, size and spacing of type. Before describing the tests carried
out and commenting on the results, it seems appropriate to give
a short account of the Library Association's concern with the provision
of books for readers with bad sight.

During recent years public librarians have been made increasingly
aware of the difficulties of the visually handicapped. Repeated
requests for books or lists of books in larger-than-normal print
have pin-pointed the problem. This interest resulted in the formation,
in 1960, of a sub-committee of the Library Association's Research
Committee – on Books for Readers with Defective Sight. The
publication of a list of books available in large print, as well as
a pilot scheme for the xerographic reproduction of sample books in
enlarged type, were discussed by the Sub-committee as possible
approaches to the problem. In 1964 a grant of £10,000 was made
by the Viscount Nuffield Auxiliary Fund to support this scheme.
At about the same time, but independently, Mr. F.A. Thorpe's
Ulverscroft Press was getting under way. It was clear that the
Ulverscroft books would in fact be carrying out the original intention
of the pilot scheme, which had been to test reactions to some
experimental books. It was decided to postpone the use of the major

1

part of the grant, and concentrate on supporting Mr. Thorpe's work by giving publicity to it, by contributing to the cost of a prospectus, by helping with the selection of titles and by assessing reactions to his books through questionnaires to librarians.

By November 1964 the Sub-committee had come to the conclusion that, although the distribution of xerographic copies might still be one means of research, the widespread distribution previously envisaged no longer seemed the best course of action. The divergent and sometimes contradictory replies to the questionnaires on the Ulverscroft books showed that a great deal of fact finding still remained to be done. On the advice of Professor Arnold Sorsby, it was decided that an investigation into the number and kind of people reading large print books would not be worthwhile. The problem of incomplete registration of partially-sighted people, and therefore inadequate information about total numbers involved, seemed to go beyond the Library Association's field of interest. A more practical approach would be an investigation into requirements in terms of print design and production. A revised scheme was therefore put up to the Nuffield Foundation.

While the exact nature of the research work was under discussion, the Sub-committee gave continued support to Mr. Thorpe's scheme and to the National Library for the Blind's plans for a Loan Collection of titles not included in the Ulverscroft Series. Also, at the end of 1965 the Library Association published their Special Subject List No. 47, *Large and Clear*.

The revised plans for research that were accepted by the Viscount Nuffield Auxiliary Fund can best be described by quoting from the 1965-66 Annual Report of the Nuffield Foundation:-

> "The (Library) Association sought the help of the Fund in connexion with an enquiry into the production of books for the partially-sighted. Of a total grant of up to £10,000, £500 was used in the early stages to distribute to public and hospital libraries free sample copies of one of a series of large type books produced by Mr. F.A. Thorpe (a retired publisher interested in blind welfare) on a non-profit making basis. The information gained through this pilot scheme decided the Library Association to use the remainder of the grant on a programme of experiments into the legibility of various type faces and the presentation of printed materials".

2.0 THE CASE FOR TYPOGRAPHIC RESEARCH

The first task in any research work is to define what ground should be covered – which aspects of the problem should be investigated, and how they should be investigated. This project, as a single and rather specialised aid to the visually handicapped, therefore had to be looked at in the general context of the whole range of education and welfare services available to the partially-sighted, and also in the particular context of work that had already been done to provide large print books. The importance of this perspective is perhaps obvious: not only was it necessary to avoid duplication of effort and to see where the gaps in information lay, but also to avoid the pitfall of carrying out an exercise, the results of which, would be difficult or impossible to put to practical use in terms of existing welfare programmes or book production methods.

2.1 Activity Before 1945

The provision of legible reading material for the partially-sighted has been considered periodically over the years, particularly by teachers and those concerned with the education and welfare of children. As early as the 1880s special large print books were being published in Germany "for children with weak sight, whose eyes must be spared" (Cohn, 1886). But the problem received relatively little attention elsewhere and for two main reasons. First of all – and understandably – effort and interest were early concentrated on the more obvious problems of those people who were considered *blind* and unable to read printed material of any kind. Secondly, medical opinion discouraged people with bad vision from using their eyes for close tasks like reading, even though their sight was not bad enough for them to be thought of as blind. As recently as the late 1930s, many medical experts still believed that the use of defective eyes could be harmful; residual vision had to be "saved" not used. In addition, economic reasons discouraged the production of special books for people unable to read normal print. The total numbers of people with severely defective and uncorrectable vision was (and still is) small in terms of a commercial publishing market. Statistics have always been incomplete, but it was estimated in 1934 that there were 6,000 partially-sighted children in England and Wales, only 2,000 of whom were receiving special education (Board of Education, 1934). Figures like these did not act as much encouragement to prospective publishers.

However, these various and negative factors did not prevent some investigations being carried out in the interests of the partially-sighted, and between the two world wars there was activity both in Great Britain and in the United States. Work in the United States resulted in the non-profit-making Clear Print Publishing Company, and in this country the National Institute for the Blind (now the Royal National Institute for the Blind), carried out a considerable amount of research into the legibility of print. Both of these schemes were concerned with the needs of children rather than of adults.

Then came the second world war, with its restrictions on book production and a considerable deterioration in the quality of paper. Scarcity of materials and increasing costs also led to a reduction in the type sizes and spacing standards used in all branches of publishing.

Since the end of the second world war, and more particularly during the last ten or fifteen years, there has been renewed interest in the idea of producing large print books. This has been due to a number of related developments in health and welfare services, and also in printing technology.

2.2 Changing Medical Opinion

One very important factor is that medical opinion has been changing over the years, and now encourages the use of residual vision in almost all cases of defective sight (Ministry of Education, 1949).

The *Crowley Report* in 1934 had pointed out that the restrictions on reading and other school work were imposed in the belief, which could not be proved or disproved, that use of the eyes had a damaging effect on the myopic eye: and that although cases of myopia might be in the majority, these restrictions were unfairly limiting on pupils who were not myopic (Board of Education, 1939). But it was not until 1947 that these traditional restrictions were lifted. Authoritative ophthalmological opinion was making it quite clear that "seeing" could of itself do no harm, that reading is not injurious to the eye, and that there is no danger in holding the print as close to the eye as is necessary for it to be focussed clearly. The possible exceptions to this being certain cases of progressive myopia with a risk of retinal detachment.

2.3 Special Education

The emphasis now placed on the needs of the partially-sighted, as distinct from those of the blind, has introduced other new trends. Special schools and classes for partially-sighted children, although in existence in Great Britain since 1908, have received impetus from the increased recognition of the partially-sighted as an individual category of the handicapped. The Education Act of 1944 recognised the distinction between really blind children (with no perception of light or with extremely defective vision), and partially-sighted children (Education Act, 1944). In 1945 Statutory Regulations described partially-sighted children thus: "... pupils who by reason of defective vision cannot follow the ordinary curriculum without detriment to their sight or to their educational development, but can be educated

4

by special methods involving sight" (Handicapped Pupils and School Health Regulations, 1945).

2.4 Registration of the Partially-Sighted

Since 1948 the voluntary registration of the partially-sighted in England and Wales has helped to draw attention to the difference in all sections of the community, between partial-sight and blindness. There were 33,545 people on the Register of Partially-Sighted Persons in 1967 (Ministry of Health, 1968). (However the number of people with defective vision who could make use of special books is at least three or four times greater than this: the problems of incomplete statistics and of defining partial-sight are discussed in Section 3.3)

The *Younghusband Report* of 1959, on Social Workers in Health and Welfare Services, while recommending greater integration of the services for handicapped people of all categories, also pointed out that the needs of the partially-sighted were often very different from those of the blind and were not necessarily any less urgent (Ministry of Health and Department of Health for Scotland, 1959).

More recently still in 1963, a Ministry of Health circular dealt specifically with the Welfare Services for the Partially-Sighted, and recommended to the local authorities responsible that their services for the partially-sighted should be made more comprehensive (Ministry of Health, 1963).

2.5 Services for the Elderly

In addition to these developments in the educational and welfare services to the partially-sighted, there has been the growing awareness over the last twenty years of the importance of services to old people. The term "an ageing society" is now so familiar that it has become almost a cliché, but it has particular relevance to those concerned with people suffering from bad eyesight. In 1967 75% of those on the Partially-Sighted Register were over 50: only 7% were under 16 (Ministry of Health, 1968). As a result of advances in medical knowledge the number of children suffering from congenital eye defects is decreasing, but there has not been a corresponding decrease in the number of old people with bad vision. Sorsby's work on the causes of blindness give authoritative evidence for this view. "This (the number of newly registered blind under the age of 50) has declined steadily to about 800 in recent years or some 7 or 8% of all new registrations. For the age group 50-69 years there has been a less definite decline over the past fifteen years, the numbers falling from around 2,700 per year in the early fifties to about 2,300 recently — about 20% of all cases. The bulk of new registrations come in the age groups over 70 years, and these new registrations have increased from about 7,000 annually to 8,000" (Ministry of Health, 1966). These figures are not surprising when it is remembered that some of the principal causes of defective vision, such as cataract and macular degeneration, are really part of the ageing process.

Thus with people living longer, a greater incidence of defective vision from these causes must be expected unless preventative measures and remedies can be found. An optimistic note has been struck in relation to the surgical treatment of cataract; better facilities have resulted in a marked decline of the incidence of this particular cause of defective vision. But while medical research continues to work on the problem of preventing blindness and partial-sight, the ancillary education and welfare services have to cope with the needs of people who suffer from these handicaps in the meantime: in assessing these needs, it is important to remember that most of the people concerned are elderly.

2.6   Importance of Book Provision

Obviously the provision of reading material is only one of many services necessary for the well-being of the partially-sighted, but it is an important one, particularly in relation to educational needs and the increasing opportunities for leisure open to retired people. At a time when scientific and technical knowledge is estimated to be doubling itself every ten or fifteen years (Licklider, 1966), everything possible should be done to help all readers (not only those with partial-sight) to assimilate the printed word more easily. Many people do more reading during their school years than at any other time in their lives, and this no doubt accounts for the concentration in the past on the problems of partially-sighted children. But whilst accepting the fact that for many adults with defective vision, reading may come low on their list of activities, the provision of books is still an important community service. The Ministry of Health circular of 1963 particularly noted the need for libraries to set aside books in large print for people with defective vision (Ministry of Health, 1963). In practice this has been hard to do because so few suitable books are available, but various technical developments in the printing industry over the last ten years or so have raised hopes of the more economic production of special books. Photographic and electrostatic techniques all seem to offer possibilities of cheaper production methods.

All these developments have resulted in various specific kinds of activity to help the partially-sighted reader and can be thought of in two related groups. One is concerned with the individual reader, and how reading aids of various kinds can help him overcome his particular disability. The other is concerned with the re-examination of the reading material itself, to see how it can be made more legible to all visually handicapped readers.

2.7   Mechanical and Optical Reading Aids

Let us first consider briefly the different kinds of reading aids that are available and how successful they have been in meeting the needs of the partially-sighted. These aids include mechanical devices such as page turners, book rests and microfilm projection units: they are used mainly in hospitals and for special cases of disablement, and are not designed especially for the partially-sighted. Books recorded on tape, although originally developed for the blind, are increasingly used by other disabled people. These aids have proved to be invaluable in many cases, but have the underlying disadvantage that the reader cannot achieve the "feel" of reading a normal book: he tends to be separated both physically and psychologically from what he is reading.

Reading aids which have been especially designed for the partially-sighted are more strictly "optical" aids, and range from simple hand magnifying lenses to sophisticated and tailor-made "low vision aids" prescribed by the ophthalmic services. These special aids should have the practical advantage that they can be used for reading anything the user chooses — the optical requirements of his particular eye condition are met by an aid made especially for him and for the task he wants to perform.

Why bother then with large print books if optical aids can do the job? The answer is not a simple one: these aids are undoubtedly helpful to many, but they do have disadvantages. In the first place they are all essentially magnifying devices, and mere enlargement of the print is not always enough to make it legible. Magnification enlarges any defects in the print, such as broken letters, "grey" printing and smudgy outlines, and cannot improve its relative blackness. Second, magnifying aids can be awkward and heavy to use, particularly for sustained periods or if the reader is elderly and has difficulty in holding the book or aid in steady focus. A considerable amount of effort and will power, if not an actual relearning process, may be required. Last, optical distortion and restricted fields of vision are difficult to eliminate. This means that, although the visibility of separate details of the print may be improved by magnification, fewer letter and word units can be seen at a time, and the normal reading mechanisms are slowed down and upset.

2.8   Specially Designed Reading Material

The other side of the coin — the design of the reading material itself — therefore does merit examination, although the provision of specially designed books should be considered as complementary to, rather than as alternative to, optical aids. There should be no suggestion that special reading material can in some way replace reading glasses.

This investigation is not the first attempt in this country to find out what makes print legible for the partially-sighted, although it is believed to be the first systematic research study. Early work between the wars at the National Institute for the Blind has already been mentioned, and will be referred to again, as will some investigations carried out more recently in schools for the partially-sighted. Tangible evidence of other work in this field is the actual publication of large print books. Mr. Thorpe's Ulverscroft Press has been a pioneer in this country and there are comparable publishing houses in the United States. A number of research studies have been carried out in the United States, mostly in connection with these publishing programmes — in planning the present investigation, this previous research work was examined, and is discussed in Section 4.0.

7

3.0 DEFINITIONS AND CONTRIBUTORY FACTORS

This project has been concerned with designing legible reading material for the partially-sighted. Before discussing relevant research work already carried out, definitions of some of the terms as used in this study are necessary. The Glossary (p. 66) gives brief definitions of specific technical terms used, but it is important at the outset to establish the meanings of certain terms which are used frequently in this report and are possibly open to ambiguous or varying interpretation.

3.1 Design

"Design" has been taken to mean the consideration of all the details which affect the appearance and structure of the finished printed product: it therefore includes all the factors concerned with the arrangement of type on paper and produced in book or magazine format — type face, size and colour, paper quality, page layout, binding and so on: it excludes the "editorial" problems of subject matter or literary style, selection of titles for book stock, etc.

3.2 Legibility

Although there is confusion about the meaning of such related terms as legibility, visibility and readability, it is now agreed by many research workers that legibility means the ease and accuracy with which comprehension of meaningful printed material takes place (Zachrisson, 1965), and this is the definition used in this study. The subsequent problems of measuring "ease", "accuracy" and "comprehension" are discussed in detail in Section 6.0.

3.3 Reading Material

Printed text material intended for continuous reading has been studied. It was important to be clear about this as the choice of valid criteria is largely dependent on the kind of material to be read.

The act of reading is not merely seeing individual printed characters: it is much more concerned with the recognition and interpretation or comprehension of whole words and groups of words. But there are different kinds of reading requiring different levels of comprehension. Compare, for example, reading road signs along a motorway and

8

reading a novel. In the first instance a few words have to be read quickly in a complicated "unrelaxed" environment. It is often unnecessary to *comprehend* all the words on the sign once it has been recognised that they are not the ones required. On the other hand, reading a novel requires a different level of concentration over a longer period. It is an extended process requiring successive recognition and comprehension of word after word. There is a physiological difference too, in that in reading a book, the reader is using the muscles of his eyes to focus on the book held perhaps 14 inches away: when reading road signs his eyes are focussed on a distant object and his eye muscles (both for accommodation and convergence) are relaxed.

It would not be surprising if different kinds of reading required different designs of printing to achieve maximum legibility. It has therefore been necessary to define clearly the kind of reading with which this research has been concerned — the reading of continuous printed text at close reading distances — books, magazine and newspaper articles. Illustrations, captions, footnotes and specialised settings for tables and reference books, etc., have not been considered: nor has "reading" material in the form of road signs, labels, specialised instructional material, television displays, etc. although many of these methods of communication are becoming increasingly important and deserve investigation.

3.4   Partially-Sighted

For the purposes of this project the term "partially-sighted" refers to anyone who, because of defective eyesight, has difficulty in reading normal sized book print, i.e. 10 - 12 point (the size used for this report). This is a much wider definition, and includes many more people, than the one used to determine whether a person can be legally registered as partially-sighted in Great Britain (Ministry of Health, 1955).

Defective or partial-sight cannot be fully corrected by spectacles. At some stage in life almost everyone needs spectacles for reading: in 1967 Britain's National Health Service supplied nearly five and a half million pairs. Spectacles can compensate for many ocular visual defects but they cannot correct visual inefficiency caused by disease. Different pathological conditions result in varying degrees and kinds of functional loss of acuity. Some patients retain normal vision when looking straight ahead, but their field of vision is impaired and they cannot perceive objects at the side. Others may have loss of vision in the centre of the field — that is the part of the eye with which fine detail like print is seen — although their peripheral vision may be relatively unimpaired. Other diseases may cause bad vision at night when illumination levels are low: yet other conditions may cause overall blurred vision or blind patches in parts of the visual field only.

In addition to the actual effect of disease at any one moment, there is also its history and prognosis. Some diseases are congenital or first effect the patient in early childhood, some occur only in middle or old age, some cause a gradual loss of acuity over a long period, while others inflict a sudden and dramatic loss of vision.

These facts emphasise some of the difficulties of defining and measuring defective vision, and go some way towards explaining the lack of reliable statistics for the incidence of visual defects. Quite apart from cases that go undiagnosed because of inadequate medical services, there is no international agreement about standards for measuring blindness: the World Health Organisation are forced to include sixty five different definitions in their statistical report on Blindness (W.H.O., 1966). Goldstein discusses in some detail the problems encountered in collecting and comparing statistical data from different countries on the incidence of visual defects (Goldstein, 1968). But he points out that even if there was adequate information on the prevalence of "blindness", this would be no measure of the prevalence of less severe ocular disorders.

Clearly statistics of defective vision can only be estimates, of varying reliability depending on the country of origin: it is fortunate that those for the United Kingdom can be considered to be relatively good. Total blindness — that is not even perception of light — afflicts less than 5% of the registered blind in England and Wales: well over half of those on the Blind Register have some degree of useful vision (Ministry of Health, 1966). According to a recent government survey, 24% of the registered blind aged 16 - 64 can see large print (Government Social Survey, 1968). In addition there are thirty thousand or so people on the Register of the Partially-Sighted (Ministry of Health, 1968) almost all of whom can read print of some sort. Taking these facts into account and also the people who could qualify but are not actually registered, the figure of 100,000 seems a conservative estimate of numbers in England and Wales who have severely defective eyesight, but who can read some print. This estimate implies an incidence of 1 in 500 of the total population: estimates by the National Society for the Prevention of Blindness Inc. suggest that in the United States the proportion may be as high as 1 in 100 (Nat. Soc. for the Prevention of Blindness, 1967). It seems reasonable to assume that the incidence in the less developed countries of Asia, Africa and South America would certainly not be lower than in the "westernised" parts of the world.

Despite uncertainty about absolute numbers and incidence rates, it is more certain that most of the partially-sighted are elderly. This is particularly true of the more developed countries where increasing numbers of people live past the age of fifty. This point has already been discussed in the previous section but is worth repeating — 75% of those on the 1967 Partially-Sighted Register in England and Wales were over 50 — only 7% were under 16 (Ministry of Health, 1968). A comparably high proportion of the visually handicapped are in the older age groups in the United States (American Foundation for the Blind, 1968).

However it is important to remember that an inability to see small print may be the only common ground between any two partially-sighted people. Apart from differences in pathological cause and duration of eye defect, differences in personal characteristics of education, social background and reading taste can be as great as in any other cross section of the community.

3.5 Identification of Contributory Factors

Reading as a visual task requires three basic elements:

(1) Object or printed display — the factors involved here can be called *Printing Characteristics.*

(2) Visual apparatus (the eye) and acquired skill of the reader — these include both physiological and psychological factors, and might be given the omnibus title of *Reader Characteristics.*

(3) *Illumination* acting as a vital link between the print and its reader.

(Another link between print and reader is *reading distance.* Because this factor has such particular significance for those with defective vision it is treated in this study as a "reader characteristic".)

Tables 1, 2 and 3 list the factors involved in each of these elements.

3.6 Illumination

It was decided at an early stage in planning the present research that the effect of changes in illumination would not be investigated. This decision was made on grounds of expediency, and not because illumination was considered an unimportant factor. It was felt that research into the problems of lighting could not be dealt with adequately within the scope of the present project. The provision of lighting facilities, and the research and development of acceptable standards have been very much the concern of the engineer. Professional organisations like the Illuminating Engineering Society in the United Kingdom, have been active in recommending lighting standards (Illum. Engin. Society, 1961). Much of this work has been concerned with the requirements of industry and public buildings and there is continuing discussion about the criteria on which such standards should be based (Weston, 1961).

In relation to the particular task of reading, the intensity of illumination has been very widely studied. The sometimes conflicting results have been discussed and evaluated by Carmichael and Dearborn (1948), and by Tinker (1965). Although the exact critical values are open to debate, experimental findings generally confirm that visual acuity of normally-sighted people increases rapidly with intensity of illumination up to 5 - 10 lumens/sq. ft. After that, the increase in acuity with increasing illumination is relatively slow and becomes hardly noticeable at illumination levels above about 35 lumens/sq. ft. (Kunz and Sleight, 1949). Tinker (1965) points out that other factors in addition to intensity of illumination have to be considered — the state of light adaptation of the eye and the distribution of the illumination, as well as the requirements of the particular task.

But although the effect of illumination on visual performance has been studied extensively in relation to the normal eye, there has been very little work with defective vision. Tinker recommends illumination levels for eyes with less than normal vision of 25 - 30 lumens/sq. ft. for normal reading, and 40 - 50 for sustained reading: for schools for partially-sighted children he suggests 50 - 60 lumens/sq. ft.

11

In order to emphasise the importance of illumination for the partially-sighted, and in the absence of direct experimental evidence, it is worthwhile drawing attention to the work that has been done in relation to illumination requirements and ageing. Even with the normal eye, the amount of light reaching the retina decreases with age (Weale, 1963). Illumination at the age of 60 is about one third of that received from the same source at the age of 20, although this effect of age is only really noticed when great visual demands are made on the observer i.e. at or near the lower limits of his visual capacity (Weston, 1962). These findings would imply that someone who is partially-sighted will be particularly susceptible to decreases in retinal illumination: not only is he likely to be elderly and therefore suffering from "natural" decreased illumination due to age, but in addition, because of his defective vision, he will be using his eyes at or near the limit of his visual capacity. This deficiency in light reaching the retina can to some extent be made up for by increasing the levels of illumination, but the performance of even the normal ageing eye cannot be completely restored in this way (Weale, 1963). The work of Weston and of Ferree and Rand has shown that levels of illumination cannot compensate entirely for adverse conditions in the viewed object or task itself i.e. small size of detail and poor contrast (Rand, 1946).

Thus, illumination is not necessarily the decisive factor in any visual task although more work should be done to determine its relative importance for the partially-sighted. Such work should consider the effect of changes in illumination, not only in relation to different visual acuities, but also in relation to different causes of defective vision (it is well known, for example, that albinos are particularly sensitive to strong light), and to different kinds of visual task.

Table 1

PRINTING CHARACTERISTICS

1. Type
    (a) face
    (b) form i.e. capitals, lower case, italics
    (c) weight i.e. boldness
    (d) size
    (e) colour — see 3f below

2. Paper
    (a) opacity
    (b) gloss i.e. shininess
    (c) colour — see 3f below

3. Spatial arrangement & layout (interrelationship of type & paper)
    (a) spacing between letters
    (b) spacing between words
    (c) spacing between lines i.e. leading
    (d) length of line i.e. measure, and justification
    (e) arrangement of type on paper i.e. margins, paragraphing, columns, facing pages, etc.
    (f) colour of type, colour of paper and contrast between the two

4. Format
    (a) page size
    (b) binding

5. Reproduction

Table 2

READER CHARACTERISTICS

1. Age
2. Sex
3. Intelligence, education & occupation
4. Reading ability & habits
5. Use of reading aids (magnifiers, etc.)
6. Reading distance
7. Visual acuity
8. Medical history: pathology, age at onset of eye defect, other disabilities
9. "Psychology" (will power, temperament, desire to read, powers of concentration, aesthetic preferences & taste, etc.)

Table 3

ILLUMINATION CHARACTERISTICS
1. Quantity
2. Quality
3. Distribution

4.0 EARLIER RESEARCH WORK

As a first step towards selecting the factors to be investigated in the present study, previous research in the field was analysed in terms of the characteristics listed in tables 1, 2 and 3. Table 4 is a summary of the factors examined in these earlier studies.

Only those studies which have been concerned specifically with legibility for the partially-sighted are included in this table. There is in addition, an extensive literature on legibility of print for normal sighted readers: it is of couse also relevant, and several bibliographies and summaries of this work are available (Medical Research Council, 1926: Tinker, 1963: National Bureau of Standards, 1967: Zachrisson, 1965: Spencer, 1968).

Before discussing the general conclusions reached and the lessons to be learnt from this earlier work with the partially-sighted, specific findings of the different studies are briefly summarised.

4.1 Specific Results

Irwin carried out objective reading tests of various serif type faces with children in Conservation of Vision Classes in the United States. He found that 24 point Century School Book and 24 point Caslon Bold were both more legible than three 30 point faces (Caslon Oldstyle, Clearface and Cloister Oldstyle) and two other 24 point faces (Caslon Light and Clearface). His results were statistically significant at the 5% level (Irwin, 1919-20).

The *(Royal) National Institute for the Blind's* investigations were subjective, based on teachers' and partially-sighted pupils' opinions: there were no statistically significant results, although it is interesting to find that one conclusion reached (albeit statistically unreliable) was that Gill Sans Bold — a sans serif face was preferred by the children to six serif faces (Caslon Bold, Goudy, Garamond, Plantin, Old Style Antique and Imprint) (RNIB, 1928-38).

Fortner found no statistically significant differences between 18 and 24 point when testing these objectively (Fortner, 1943).

The study carried out by *Eakin, Pratt and McFarland* in 1952 was also unable to come to any statistically significant conclusions in testing 12, 18 and 24 point types objectively, although the investigators suggest that because more visually handicapped children were able to read 24 point than either 18 or 12 point, the larger size is preferable (Eakin, Pratt and McFarland, 1961).

14

Table 4   *ANALYSIS OF PREVIOUS RESEARCH*

	IRWIN 1919-20	RNIB 1928-38	FORTNER 1943	EAKIN 1961	NOLAN 1959-61	BABLOLA 1961	TREDREA 1964	PRINCE 1957-66	BIRCH 1966
PRINTING									
1 Type									
a. face	✓	✓			✓		✓	✓	
b. form								✓	
c. weight									
d. size	✓	✓	✓	✓	✓			✓	✓
2 Paper									
a. opacity									
b. gloss									
3 Spacing									
a. between letters	✓							✓	
b. " words	✓							✓	
c. " lines	✓						✓		
d. length of line & justification							✓		
e. arrangement of type on paper									
f. colour of type & paper		✓			✓	✓		✓	
4 Format									
a. page size									
b. binding									
5 Reproduction									
READERS									
1 Age {a = children / b = adults}	a	a	a	a	a	b	a	a & b	a
2 Sex								✓	✓
3 Intelligence etc.					✓		✓	✓	✓
4 Reading ability				✓			✓		✓
5 Use of reading aids									
6 Reading distance controlled	+								+
7 Visual acuity	*	*	*	*	*	φ	*	†	*
8 Medical history	✓		✓				✓	✓	✓
9 "Psychology"	✓	✓	✓			✓	✓		✓
ILLUMINATION controlled			✓	✓		✓		✓	

*   all subjects were pupils in partially-sighted schools or classes.

†   in his earlier work, Prince's subjects were given simulated vision defects, but in his main report to the American Library Association his subjects were actually partially-sighted.

+   reading distance measured but not controlled.

φ   vision defects simulated.

Nolan found a common serif type (Antique Oldstyle) to be significantly more legible, at the 5% level, than a sans serif type (Metrolite Medium): he found no differences between 18 and 24 point (Nolan, 1959).

Bablola found that white lettering on a black background was helpful for people with poor visual acuity but his tests were concerned with seeing single characters e.g. car number plates, and not with normal continuous reading (Bablola, 1961).

Tredrea's investigations did not produce any statistically significant results, although the study did suggest that considerable enlargement of print for older partially-sighted children is unnecessary (Tredrea, 1964).

Prince's work has probably been the most searching previous investigation. Apart from Bablola, who was an optician, Prince is the only worker in this field who has approached the problem from the optical standpoint: the other investigators have all been primarily concerned as teachers or otherwise closely connected with the education of partially-sighted children. Prince's various studies have dealt mainly with the development of a letter style specially designed to meet the theoretical optical needs of readers – both adults and children – with bad vision, but his practical tests have shown that this design (a sans serif) is less legible than a commonly used serif face (Baskerville) (Prince, 1966).

Birch and his associates were primarily concerned with the overall problems of educational standards and achievement of visually handicapped children: his tests with type sizes were inconclusive (Birch, Tisdall, Peabody and Sterrett, 1966).

4.2   Importance of Experimental Method

What could one conclude from this lack of decisive results to guide further work? It would not be correct to assume that because no conclusive results have been found, there are none to find. Very few of the accounts of this earlier work give adequate descriptions of methodological procedures – experimental conditions like illumination were often not controlled or standardised, comparability of reader groups and typographic variables were not established, and test criteria were sometimes invalid. For example, the sizes of the type faces tested by Irwin were not compared systematically – 24 point Century School Book appears more or less the same visual size as 30 point Caslon Oldstyle when printed. It is thus impossible to draw any general conclusions about size as a factor from this study. Fortner used blink-rate as a criterion of legibility, and this is likely to be a particularly dubious method for use with the abnormal eye. Eakin and his colleagues used a fixed reading distance of 14", which again could be said to be invalid for readers with very poor vision. In other words, much of the earlier work suffered from inadequate or misguided experimental control.

The wide variation, in cause of defective vision and in the amount of remaining vision, makes it likely that there are no absolutely hard and fast rules governing legibility standards for the partially-sighted.

16

However, the previous work in this field has not gone very far towards formulating even the most generalised guide lines: the one important lesson learnt from it is more the importance of a well-conceived experimental design than facts about legible print standards.

The methodological problems involved in achieving statistically valid and reliable results from objective tests are discussed in detail in Section 6.0.

4.3 Printing Characteristics Studied

Table 4 shows that only some of the printing characteristics in table 1 had been examined in the earlier studies. Even if the validity of the work already done on size and style of type were to be accepted, there would remain several other important factors that had not been examined — in particular those concerned with spacing and layout.

4.4 Concentration on Children's Needs

It is interesting that most of the previous work was in relation to children: Prince's investigations have been the only ones to look at the problems of the partially-sighted adult. Children's needs are of course important — reading is a basic key to education — but there is a case to be made for looking more thoroughly into the difficulties of adult readers and concentrating new work on their requirements. There are two reasons to support this suggestion. First of all, as already discussed, there are many more adults than children with defective vision, and this is of course important from any would-be publisher's point of view. In the second place, and more important from the experimental and research point of view, the lack of results from the earlier work may have been just because children, and not adults, were being studied. Children usually retain the accommodative powers of their eye muscles: this can help offset some of the effects of defective vision by making focussing on very close objects possible. Also they have never known what it is to have good eyesight, and are generally adaptable and flexible under even the most handicapping circumstances. All this is in contrast to most partially-sighted adults who, in addition to losing powers of accommodation with increasing age, have to cope with deteriorating vision after many years of normal sight.

4.5 Translating Research Results into Print Production

Lastly, given theoretically sound results, findings must be turned to practical use by being related to practical printing and publishing production. Some of the previous studies were carried out by research workers expert in education or ophthalmology or optics, but who were unfamiliar with technical printing terminology and practice. Although experimental methods may mean that printing practice has to be overridden in designing sample printings for testing, final conclusions must be translated back into terms that the printer understands if they are to have any chance of acceptance and implementation.

Part II

Research Aims and Methodology

5.0 PROPOSALS FOR THE LIBRARY ASSOCIATION RESEARCH PROJECT

The exploratory investigation into the general field of services for the partially-sighted and into the particular area of previous large print research, was supplemented by very constructive discussions with experts in the relevant fields of education, welfare, ophthalmology, optics, printing and experimental method.

It was then decided to carry out a series of objective tests to investigate the effect on legibility of variations in

(a) *Type Face*

(b) *Type Weight*

(c) *Type Size*   and

(d) *Type Spacing* – varying inter letter, inter word and inter line spacing.

The tests were to be carried out with two groups of partially-sighted readers – one group of adults, and another smaller group of children. The numbers in each group were to be large enough to give reasonable confidence in any results.

Each subject was to be interviewed and asked to read aloud, under standard illumination, short paragraphs printed in the different styles. (Specimen test cards are included in Appendix A).

The reading performances, measured by time taken and mistakes made, were then to be analysed by computer, using multiple regression techniques. Other data were to be collected in the course of each interview and used in the analysis. By using a carefully controlled experimental design it was hoped that this statistical analysis would provide reliable and valid information about the relative importance of different print factors.

The section which follows contains a full discussion on the choice of typographic factors tested, word content of test passages, sample of readers, experimental procedures followed, and methods of analysis used.

6.0 METHODOLOGY

The purpose of the tests was to study the effect of variations in "printing characteristics" on the ease with which partially-sighted readers were able to read continuous text. The purpose was *not* to test the intelligence of the partially-sighted or to carry out a survey of reading taste or use of optical aids, although account was taken of these and other factors in attempting to reach valid conclusions about the legibility of the print being tested.

6.1 Approach to Experimental Method

The effective design of reading material depends on the consideration of all the factors listed in Table 1. Exact specifications may not always be the result of a conscious choice on the part of the designer, and are just as likely to be determined by convention, tradition, fashion or economics. Nevertheless they have to be drawn up for every one of these factors. For example, however unimportant it may be for a particular purpose, the length of line has to be specified in some way, the colour of paper chosen (even if it's only "white"), a particular type face (out of the thousands available) selected, and so on. More often than not, the requirements of one factor will control another – the type size and page size will determine the bulk and weight of the book, the type design may determine the "leading". If all these factors have to be considered, what is the point of trying to isolate a few of them for special investigation? The answer is that although they all play some part in the total design, we do not always know how big a part each factor plays in relation to another – we do not know which factors are the most important. If it were possible to put these factors into some sort of order of priority, the task of designing or choosing print for the normally-sighted reader, as well as for the partially-sighted, would be easier. If it were known for example that the colour of the print and paper, within certain limits, made little or no difference to legibility, or that subtle differences between type faces had little effect compared with say, extra spacing between the words, we would be on much sounder ground in recommending print design. As it is, few firm facts are known about the problem as it relates to partially-sighted readers. A systematic analysis of the factors involved therefore was worthwhile and was the purpose of the present investigation; but it is important to remember that such an approach is only a means to an end. Synthesis must follow the analysis of the individual factors. The total result of a design for print is much more than a sum of its different parts, and the interaction between the separate printing factors is important. This means that an analysis of the separate parts cannot necessarily account for the combined effect of various factors.

It is important to remember that the effectiveness of the total design is also influenced by factors extraneous to the physical characteristics of ink on paper. The subject matter of the print, the reader, and his purpose in reading are all relevant. This has been put in very practical and salutory terms by Prince as one of his conclusions to his report to the American Library Association – "The results could serve as an outstanding example of the caution with which one should consider applying controlled laboratory findings to people in their natural surroundings" (Prince, 1966). The history of legibility research with its conflicting and statistically unreliable findings, bears witness to the methodological difficulties in this field, and in work with partially-sighted readers in particular, inadequate experimental procedures have been a main cause of confusion. Successful test methods have not yet been established and so new work inevitably has to be concerned with problems of methodology (i.e. how to test), as well as what to test. The choice of printing characteristics to be tested in this investigation was influenced in some degree therefore, by the test methods that could be devised.

The choice of test procedures was thus a compromise between

(a) testing the interaction of as many different printing characteristics as possible

(b) keeping the number of tests within manageable limits, and

(c) making the tests valid and "relateable" to a normal reading situation.

In an effort to obtain consistent results it was decided at the outset that the tests should be administered by the same person. (There were too many other variables in the situation, without adding the possibility of interviewer inconsistency). This put some sort of limit on the number of subjects that it would be practical to test individually. Assuming that each test might take about 30 minutes, it seemed reasonable to undertake about 300 interviews. The length of interview – 30 mins. – was also based on the likelihood of many of the subjects being elderly and all of them handicapped, and unused to carrying out lengthy and complicated tests under controlled conditions. Also, because the effort required to carry out the tests might be considerable in many cases, it was decided that each subject should be asked to read four tests only.

6.2 Typographic Factors to be Tested

On the basis therefore of about 300 subjects, each reading four tests, an experiment was designed to test 32 different print combinations. Details of the methodological design used are discussed in Section 6.6. The typographic variables making up the 32 different combinations were to be:

Type Face in 2 variations – a serif and a sans serif (in lower case)

Type Weight in 2 variations – a bold and a medium

Type Size in 2 variations – the actual sizes tested to depend on the reading acuity of each reader – see Section 6.3

Type Spacing (inter letter, inter word, inter line) in 4 variations.

i.e. a total of 2 × 2 × 4 × 2 = 32 combinations.

These factors were selected from the list of Printing Characteristics in Table 1 as being the most worthwhile and logical ones to test first, and as being the most susceptible to simple testing and requiring a minimum of type setting. (Printing costs can be an expensive item in this field of research).

Of the factors not selected for the tests, most are concerned with overall page arrangement and layout, and their examination would logically seem to follow, rather than precede, tests on type face, size and weight. The one factor that was not selected and yet would have fitted into an initial investigation, is that of letter form – capitals (upper case), lower case, and italic letters – all the tests of type face, size and weight were to be in normal upper and lower case. However there is reasonable agreement between earlier legibility studies that an "all capitals" style retards normal reading (Tinker, 1963). The probable explanation for this is, that when continuous text is read, the word unit counts more than the individual letters, and the visual form of words in lower case is more easily recognised than words in capitals. These earlier studies have been with normal sighted readers and although one might expect different results with children and adults with congenitally defective vision, it would be reasonable to believe that for those partially-sighted adults losing their sight later in life, the advantages of lower case letters would still hold good. Prince's studies support this view (Prince, 1966).

Similarly, evidence on the use of italics shows that normal readers read italics more slowly (Tinker, 1963). One would expect the italic form to be even more difficult for the partially-sighted reader, as it is usually relatively light in weight, fussy in design and, when mixed with ordinary lower case, tends to be smaller in "appearing" size.

On grounds of common sense it seemed that the use of either "all capitals" or "all italics" is not likely to improve legibility for the partially-sighted. A contributory, although not decisive, argument is that it is not common practice to print continuous text in either of these forms. This means that there is the problem of unfamiliarity on the part of the reader, as well as reluctance on the part of the printer, to contend with. It was decided therefore not to test these variations in letter form.

6.3 Specifications of Test Printings

The basic principles underlying the typographic specifications of variables to be tested were as follows:

1. *The typographic differences being tested should be large ones,* and judged by some design standards, rather crude. This is not to say that more subtle differences may not also be important and effective in some instances, but is more in acknowledgement of the fact that in order to obtain objectively measureable differences in performance, extreme conditions often have to be compared. If legibility is a continuous progression from the totally illegible at one end of the

scale, to the optimum at the other, performance can obviously be measured at any point along the curve or line between these two points. But if two points rather close together on the scale are compared, the resulting performances may be so similar that a real difference can be hidden by random variability. Another point relevant in the particular context of partially-sighted readers is the obvious one of defective visual acuity. Legibility depends in the first instance on the physical ability of the eye to *see* the print by means of stimulation of the retina at the back of the eye. Without this ability none of the other important but subsequent processes (interpretation by the brain, etc.) can begin to complete the perceptive processes involved in *reading*. Visual acuity can be defined as the ability of the eye to distinguish fine detail, i.e. small differences; its measurement includes an evaluation of brightness discrimination as well as of form vision. A partially-sighted person who by definition has an abnormally poor visual acuity, must therefore be presented with correspondingly greater differences if he is to be able to distinguish between them, or if his performance is to reflect significant differences between conditions.

2. *Specifications should be in terms of current printing practice.*
That is to say that type faces and measurements used in the printing trade should be the basis of the experiments. This is not to presuppose that existing type designs and conventions cannot or should not be radically altered for the use of the partially-sighted. It is rather a more practical and economic approach to finding out what is wrong with present practice before considering re-design. There is as yet no very clear evidence to suggest that the wide selection of existing designs (over a thousand faces are listed in the 1958 edition of *An Encyclopaedia of Type Faces* published by the Blandford Press) does not offer considerable scope for investigation and possibilities for improvement. There is some evidence in fact to suggest the contrary i.e. that departures from current practice can be a hindrance rather than a help. Burt came to the conclusion that one of the most powerful factors affecting legibility for the normally-sighted is habit: people read most easily those type faces to which they are most accustomed (Burt, 1960). Prince, from his work with partially-sighted adults, came to the conclusion that when strong behaviour patterns have been well established before deterioration in vision, conventional types, although not necessarily clearly seen in detail, are read more easily than specially designed ones (Prince, 1966).

In addition to these theoretical arguments, there is an economic argument in favour of making as much use as possible of present practice. The design of a new type face involves high costs and does not in itself guarantee acceptance and usage by printers.

3. *The type faces tested should be selected for real comparability.*
The inconclusiveness and lack of general applicability of many legibility studies has been because it is so difficult to make objective comparisons between type faces. The subtle differences in design seem to make for equally subtle and hard to define differences in legibility. The complications and confusions of printers' measurements and terminology (e.g. point size, x-height), have bemused the experimental psychologist and often invalidated his results. If 12 point Times New Roman is not really the same size as 12 point Caslon, how can one

22

conclude anything about size as a typographic factor? If Baskerville Bold looks bolder than Garamond Bold, how can one generalise about the effect of boldness as a factor? This problem of comparability must be faced if there is to be any chance of discovering valid facts about the particular type faces, and then reaching conclusions about typographic factors in general.

With these three principles in mind, the printing characteristics to be tested — face, weight, size and spacing — were considered.

Face — Plantin and Gill Sans were selected.

These type faces were chosen for the following reasons:

1. They could be considered as representative examples of two of the main categories of type face design — Plantin as a serif face and Gill Sans as a sans serif face.

2. By subjective standards they are reasonably legible for text settings, without any wild eccentricities of design.

3. They are comparable with each other in appearing size, x-height and width of letter; and also in general "weight" or "colour", although this is a difficult factor to compare as, by definition, the serif face is made up of strokes of varying thickness while the strokes of a sans serif are all more or less the same thickness. The checking for comparability was made easier and more accurate by using the unit system of measurement developed by the Monotype Corporation and described in *Scientific Copyfitting* (Monotype Corp. Ltd, 1966).

4. Each face is available in different weights, so comparisons between medium and bold versions of the same face can be made, as well as between the two faces.

5. The faces are available on filmsetting equipment which meant that exact control of sizes and spacing could be achieved.

Weight (boldness)

Light, medium and bold versions of both Plantin and Gill Sans are available. Only the medium and bold were selected for the tests. On common-sense grounds the light versions would appear to be particularly unsuitable for partially-sighted readers and were therefore not tested. The medium (in common use for normal text setting) and the bold versions contrast with each other, and seemed to be a logical starting point in discovering the importance of boldness for partially-sighted readers.

Size

This investigation is concerned with type sizes between about 12 point (normal text size) and 24 point. Sizes larger than 24 point are out of the question for any regular practical production purpose. The sizes 12, 14, 16, 18, 20 and 24 point were to be tested: these six steps have the advantage of being identifiable in terms of printers' point sizes.

It is possible that this progression errs on the side of having too many steps and that 4 or 5 would be more appropriate than 6. Psychologists are agreed that the amount that has to be added to any stimulus to

produce a detectable difference is relative to what is already there
(Stevens, 1951). This would suggest that it is necessary to increase
18 point type, say, by a greater amount than 12 point to observe the
same effect on performance. Work on the design of ophthalmic test
types tends to confirm that this general law of psychophysics does
apply to visual stimuli (Bennett, 1965). A geometric rather than an
arithmetic progression might therefore be more appropriate. Bennett
discusses the various progressions that are in use or proposed for use
in test types. In relation to printers' type sizes, a geometric
progression with a ratio of 1:2·25 for example, would give a progression
of 12 point, 15 point, $18\frac{3}{4}$ point and $23\frac{1}{2}$ point i.e. 4 steps. A test type
in current use for measuring reading acuity uses 4 steps, going from
12 to 14 to 18 to 24 point, but it is generally recognised that this
progression does not include enough steps for satisfactory assessment
of bad vision (see also Section 6.5). It therefore seemed more sensible
to include more steps in the type size progression to be tested: the
differences between the steps (at least 2 points) are still quite large
in printers' terms.

It is important to emphasise here that the object of the tests was not to
determine absolute sizes for optimal legibility, but rather to establish
the relative importance of size, compared with the other factors of
face, weight and spacing. In effect the tests examined only 2 variations
in size – a "larger" and a "smaller": each reader was given tests
nearest to his visual threshold (see Section 6.5). If he could only just
see 14 point on the ophthalmic test chart, for example, he would be
given typographic tests in 12 and 14 point; if he could just see 20 point,
the tests would be in 18 and 20 point. It was anticipated that the
readers would differ widely in reading acuity and that it would therefore
be necessary to have sets of tests in different size groups available –
12 and 14 point, 14 and 16 point, 16 and 18 point, 18 and 20 point,
20 and 24 point.

Spacing

Spacings *within* a block of print were to be considered for these tests
i.e. spacing between the letters, between the words, and between the
lines (leading). The special requirements of paragraph spacing and
the spacing involved in overall page layout e.g. margins, were not to
be tested: nor were problems of "justification". Justification means
that the regular spacing between words is adjusted so that each line in
a block of type is the same length, and the right hand side as well as
the left hand side of the block is even. It is extremely hard to measure
the effect of changing inter-word spacing in justified printing, because
the spacing between the words is by definition irregular and the
hyphenation of words introduces an extraneous variable. Because of
these problems it was decided to use unjustified settings for the tests,
although efforts were made to prevent too much variation in line length.
This point concerning the visual appearance and word content of the
test printings is discussed in Section 6.9.

It was decided that in examining the effect of spacing, the simplest
method would be to look at just 2 different amounts of spacing between
letters, 2 between words and 2 between lines. The aim of the tests
was not to find the *amount* of spacing that affected legibility, but rather
to find out what variations in *kind* of spacing had a significant effect.

To make a valid assessment, the interaction of the different kinds of
spacing i.e. letter, word and line, have to be considered: to examine
fully two variations in each it would be necessary to test the 8 different
combinations shown in Table 5.

Table 5

INTERACTION OF VARIATIONS IN SPACING

		inter letter space	inter word space	inter line space
combination	a)	1	1	1
"	b)	2	1	1
"	c)	1	2	1
"	d)	2	2	1
"	e)	1	1	2
"	f)	2	1	2
"	g)	1	2	2
"	h)	2	2	2

Within the limiting framework of the investigation discussed in Section
6.2, eight combinations were too many to test. It was necessary to
select four only. Anyway several of the combinations did not seem
worth investigating objectively – common sense suggested that some
combinations would almost certainly be less legible than others. The
variations thus eliminated were (b) and (f), on the grounds that an
increase in inter letter space, *without* an increase in inter word space,
would tend to make reading more difficult by making the word units
(which are the normal reading units), run into each other. Combinations
(g) and (h) were not to be examined in the tests either because of the
need to limit the number of combinations to be tested: these combinations
might well be important but it seemed more logical to test them after
the others.

In deciding the exact spacing specifications, it seemed sensible to take
(a) as a standard and specify it in terms of what might be accepted as
standard printing practice. By using film-setting as the method of
composition, it was possible to ensure that these variations in spacings
were proportionate from size to size – difficult or impossible to achieve
using traditional hot metal methods.

Final Specifications

The composition of the type was done on a Monophoto filmsetter using
the unit system of spacing measurement (Monotype Corp. Ltd, 1966).
Specimens of the test printings are included in Appendix A. They were
printed by offset lithography on 3 sheet Foxhunter Matt Twin Wire
Super White Board. As neither colour of ink nor paper were being
examined, the main requirement for these factors was that they should
be kept constant for all the tests. For ease of administering the tests,
a stiff light board was used rather than paper, so that the sheets would
remain flat while being read. The board used had low reflectance value
and was opaque, so problems of glare and show-through did not arise.

25

The sheets were printed on one side only and trimmed to the following sizes:

12, 14, 16, 18pt sizes - $5\frac{1}{2} \times 8\frac{3}{4}$".
20, 24pt sizes - $8\frac{3}{8} \times 11$".

The detailed specifications are shown in Table 6 opposite.

6.4   Choice of Test Criteria

The present study was an investigation of the relationship between design of print and visual function in continuous text reading: it was not concerned with the mental functions of the reader. Any test method used had to try to distinguish between these two functions − visual and mental − although this is a distinction which is frequently difficult to make in analysing normal reading.

It is possible that readers with subnormal vision use different kinds of eye movements from readers with normal vision, but not enough is known about this for it to contribute to the design of the methods used in this present study. It seemed sensible to try to stimulate normal continuous reading conditions i.e. use of near point of vision, saccadic eye movements (movements consisting of a series of jumps and fixations and regression along lines of print) and visual span.

The following ten methods have been used in the past as criteria of legibility for readers with normal vision:

1. Speed of Perception
2. Distance of Perception
3. Peripheral Vision Perception
4. Visibility
5. Reflex Blink Rate
6. Eye Movements
7. Fatigue measurement
8. Binocular rivalry
9. Rate of work
10. Readers' opinions.

No single one of these methods has complete advantage over the others, and there has been continuing discussion over the years about which methods produce valid results (Tinker, 1963; Zachrisson, 1965). The basic problem is to select criteria which can be measured objectively and at the same time reflect real differences in legibility. Before deciding on the criteria to be used in this study, each of the methods listed above was considered in relation to partially-sighted readers.

Methods 1 and 2 were dismissed because they do not measure reading under normal viewing conditions. 1 relies on short exposure of the object, specifically not allowing eye movements to function normally: 2 uses viewing distances much greater than those used for normal near point reading. Methods 3, 5, 6 and 8 were also ruled out because they depend on measuring physiological and muscular functions: these functions are inadequately understood in the normal eye, so it seemed unwise to use them as criteria for studies with the abnormal eye. 10 is a method that has been relatively unsuccessful in producing results

26

Table 6

TYPOGRAPHIC SPECIFICATIONS OF TEST PRINTINGS
(specimens included in Appendix A)

FACE	WEIGHT	SIZE	SPACING
			each in 4 different spacings:-
			1 - "standard"
			(a) in Table 5
			i.e. normal letter space,
			normal word space
			(5 units),
		each in	normal line space
			(no leading).
		12 point	
			2 - (d) in Table 5
	Medium		i.e. increased letter
	(Monotype 262)		space (2 units),
Gill Sans			increased word
	Bold	14 "	space (12 units),
	(Monotype 275)		normal line space
		16 "	(no leading).
			3 - (c) in Table 5
			i.e. normal letter space,
			increased word space
		18 "	(9 units),
			normal line space
	Medium		(no leading).
	(Monotype 110)		
			4 - (e) in Table 5
Plantin		20 "	i.e. normal letter space,
	Bold		normal word space
	(Monotype 194)		(5 units),
		24 "	increased line space
			proportionate to
			point size thus:-
			3 pt. leading for 12 pt.
			$3\frac{1}{2}$" " " 14 "
			4 " " " 16 "
			$4\frac{1}{2}$" " " 18 "
			5 " " " 20 "
			6 " " " 24 "

with normal readers and is, by definition, subjective: however, because
it might be of some interest in itself, it was decided to collect readers'
opinions as a secondary criterion in the investigation. Method 7 (the
measurement of fatigue) might seem to be an especially good criterion
to use with people who are necessarily reading with visual difficulty
anyway, but methodological studies have so far failed to find an adequate
and practical means of measuring fatigue (Carmichael & Dearborn, 1948).

This left Methods 4 (Visibility) and 9 (Rate of work). Visibility criteria
would seem to be appropriate for the study of subnormal vision in that
it is concerned to measure vision thresholds. The normally-sighted
do not usually read particularly near their visual threshold and so this
method may not be valid for them: but the partially-sighted do have to
read at their threshold, or at least much nearer to it than the normally-
sighted, and so the method would seem more suitable. The principal
investigators using this criteria have used the Luckeish-Moss Visibility

Meter (Luckeish & Moss, 1935), but this instrument is not designed for testing continuous text reading. However it was decided to use some of the basic ideas behind visibility measurements for the present study, and in combination with Method 9 (Rate of work). Measurement of rate of work, in some form or other, is now generally accepted as one of the most valid criteria. It can be used to measure continuous reading and, by taking into account errors made as well as reading speed, is concerned with comprehension. (The importance of comprehension in reading has been discussed in Section 3.3).

The combination of these two ways of measurement resulted in the methods used in this study. The tests were designed to determine first the visual threshold of each reader, in terms of the smallest print they could see; and then to have them read four test passages at or around this threshold size. These test passages would each be printed differently, illustrating the typographic variations that were being examined. Differences in reading performances, based on time taken and errors made, should then reflect the differences in the typography. The typographic variations that were to be tested have already been described: the determination of the visual threshold and the word content of the test passages are now discussed.

6.5   Determination of Visual Threshold and Acuity

It was necessary to determine the visual threshold of each subject to decide the appropriate sizes for the reading tests: it was also necessary to be able to correlate the performances with some form of standard measurement of visual acuity. The screening methods used had to

1. Be acceptable as standard ophthalmic practice.
2. Be capable of being carried out by a lay investigator.
3. Be simple and quick to carry out in a variety of non-clinical locations.
4. Be capable of measuring *reading* acuity accurately, without biasing results on the typographic tests.

The following methods of measurement were used:

Distance Vision

A standard Snellen chart at 6 metres (or at closer distances with a mirror when necessary) was used. The acuity of both eyes together using current spectacle correction, was recorded. (It was unnecessary in the context of this research to attempt to record the acuity of each eye separately.)

The Snellen chart used is illustrated in Appendix B, and corresponds quite closely to the proposals of the British Standards Institution Committee on Test Types, in respect of letter proportions and size.

Near Vision

(a) a reduced Snellen chart used at 35cms (and with current spectacle correction) illustrated in Appendix B.
(b) a reading test type used at 35cms (and with current spectacle correction) illustrated in Appendix B.

28

Both these charts comply with the recommendations on Reading Test Types made by the Faculty of Ophthalmologists (Law, 1952).

(c) the same reading test type as (b), but at a distance found most comfortable by the subject and using spectacle and or magnifying aids if necessary.

Near vision was recorded for both eyes together.

The standard Snellen charts for distance vision, and the Faculty recommendations for Reading Types are usually considered by ophthalmologists and opticians to be inadequate for screening subnormal vision – there is only one step, at 6/36, on the Snellen Scale between 6/24 and 6/60; and the Faculty Chart sizes jump from N14 (the printer's 14 point), to N18 (18 point), to N24 (24 point). However, existing charts have been used for this study, with a slight modification. Some intermediate sizes were added to the Faculty chart so that visual thresholds could be measured more accurately. The introduction of these extra steps in no way detracts from using the charts for standard measurements.

The type face used for the Faculty Chart is Times New Roman. It might be argued that the use of this immediately before the typographic tests might bias results: transfer effects in this kind of experiment are difficult to control (Poulton & Freeman, 1966). However, it was desirable to use the standard chart to measure reading thresholds, and it was hoped that transfer effects would be minimised by carrying out the screening at the beginning of the interview, i.e. about 20 minutes before carrying out the reading tests.

6.6   **Experimental Design**

The importance of experimental method has been discussed in Section 4.2 and the general approach used in this study in Section 6.1.: the typographic factors tested – face, weight, size and spacing – have been discussed in Section 6.2.

The experimental design used was aimed to be balanced in such a way that each of the 32 possible combinations of face, weight, size and spacing, would occur equally often: and also that each of these variables would occur equally often in the first, second, third and fourth positions in the order in which the passages were read. It was also planned that each subject should have two passages in each face, weight and size and one in each of the four spacings being tested.

This was achieved by adopting a plan based upon a series of graeco-latin squares. 144 subjects were needed to satisfy this design but it was decided to replicate it to improve the confidence limits of any results, and so a total of 288 subjects was therefore tested. Each subject read 4 passages, resulting in 1152 readings. Thus each of the 32 combinations were read 36 times.

Within the framework of this design, randomisation was used for the final allocation of typographic combinations to particular subjects. This ensured that additional factors, not controlled or balanced, did not produce any systematic bias in the results.

In the event two errors were made, one in the design and one in carrying it out, resulting in a slight imperfection in the balance of the design. However, the use of multiple regression, instead of the originally planned analysis of variance, means that this imperfection has been allowed for.

In addition to the 288 adults, further tests were made, using a suitable fraction of the complete design, with a sample of 48 children. The smaller size of the sample of course gave wider confidence limits to the results of the children's performances, but, for reasons discussed in Section 4.4, the study was concentrating on the needs of adults and so it was felt that a small sample of children would be adequate.

6.7   Sample of Readers

The subjects (reader sample) who carried out the tests were in two groups:

(a)   288 partially-sighted adults, all over 18, who were contacted through welfare departments and associations. They were all volunteers, not a pre-selected sample and were interviewed and tested "on location" in different parts of England, usually in a small room on welfare club premises.

(b)   48 children, all with a reading age of at least 11-12, who were interviewed at schools for the partially-sighted.

All the readers had one thing in common – defective vision, (although as discussed earlier, even this characteristic means different things for different people). The purpose of the tests was to try to find common ground in legibility requirements between people with partial-sight, and it was hoped that some of the basic effects of defective vision would be dominating enough to override effects of other characteristics such as age, education, reading habits and so on. The object of ascertaining the reading vision threshold for each subject was to try to make sure that the tests were read at comparable "vision levels", even though there would be a range of visual acuity (as measured by standard Snellen Charts) amongst the readers.

But there was the possibility that characteristics not related to visual acuity would influence the tests, and so it was desirable to be able to analyse the results in terms of sub-groups of the total reader sample. In order to be able to sub-divide the total group according to other criteria, and also to be able to check the representativeness of the readers, additional information was collected. A questionnaire was completed for each reader by the interviewer. The same person carried out all the interviews to help eliminate inconsistency in interview procedures. Copies of the questionnaires used are included in Appendix C.

6.8   Test Order

The order in which tests are performed by any one subject may have a significant effect on results. There can be a continuous improvement in performance unrelated to typographic differences between the first and last tests due to practice, or there can be a falling off in performance due to fatigue or boredom. There can also be asymmetrical transfer effects where the performance on a test is affected by the particular test that precedes it i. e. performance with a type face may depend upon which type face was used for the preceding test (Poulton & Freeman, 1966). Since test order was balanced in the experimental design, such effects were allowed for.

6.9 Word Content of Test Passages

One of the most important extraneous variables in legibility tests is that of the letter and word content of the passages used for testing the typographic variables. It is obviously difficult to eliminate this factor: the best that can be done is to balance the word content in such a way that it does not of itself bias the results.

Complete control of word content in this study would have required either, testing all 32 typographic variables in all of 32 different word contents (i. e. 1024 test specimens) which was clearly impractical, or, using the same four text passages for each subject which would have required each passage to be available in each style of type (i. e. 384 test specimens) which was an excessive amount of type setting. Both of these ways of ensuring lack of bias in word content seemed extravagant and unmanageable. The alternative was to use a different word content for each of the 32 typographic variables being tested, and eliminate bias by standardising the word contents in some way.

Existing reading tests were examined, but all seemed to have major disadvantages – most of them are designed for children's rather than adults' vocabulary, and many of them have been designed with American word usage. One of the most serious difficulties was that no existing tests provided enough standardised material for the 32 tests. Special passages therefore had to be composed, and in their preparation the following points were borne in mind:

1. The tests were to try to stimulate normal reading by making use of the same physiological and mechanical functions.
    This meant that the test passages had to be some form of continuous text, and not just nonsensical or isolated words and letters.

2. The tests had to be as short as possible, to minimise both printing costs and the time and effort required from the subjects.

3. The tests had to be capable of being read aloud, making it possible to score performances direct from the readings. In view of the readers involved (handicapped, and often frail and elderly), complicated ranking methods based on answers to questions on the test readings seemed undesirable. Oral reading does introduce different and additional factors compared with normal silent reading and in particular absolute reading speeds can be very different, but it seemed reasonable to believe that *relative* performance on the different tests would not be affected.

4. The tests had to be valid tests of the visual and not the mental ability of the reader. Partially-sighted readers obviously include a wide range of intelligence, education, reading habits, etc. and at the same time it is known that every reader, no matter of what

intelligence, makes use of contextual clues enabling him to read without actually seeing all the words or letters. As the purpose of these tests was to examine the effect of physiological differences rather than mental ones, it was extremely important to use a form of test which would eliminate, as far as possible, the use of contextual clues.

Word Selection

Test passages were therefore made up of semantically anomalous random sentences, for example "Hungry bridges describe expensive farmers". Although they are composed of real words and are grammatical (in the sequence adjective, noun, verb, adjective, noun) they are meaningless in the sense of the reader being able to make use of clues of context.

It has been shown that the intelligibility of strings of English words depends at least in part on their conformity to the linguistic rules known to the reader (Marks and Miller, 1964). When strings of words follow these rules, perceptual processing is made easier. Intelligibility is highest for meaningful grammatical sentences, lower for grammatical but meaningless sentences, and lowest for ungrammatical strings of words. In constructing passages for the legibility tests, it was felt that meaningless but grammatical sentences might be a satisfactory compromise. In reading such sentences, the perceptual element of intelligibility or comprehension associated with normal reading processes would be retained to some degree at least, and yet the contextual clues would be at a minimum. It was hoped that following a brief explanation by the interviewer, these sentences would be read using the mechanisms of normal reading. If a word was read aloud correctly there was a good chance that the eye had actually *seen* it, and not that the brain had interpreted it from the context. Of course contextual clues do play a part in single word recognition as well and these are not eliminated if real words are used, but it was felt that to use nothing but nonsense for the tests was too far removed from normal reading to be of value.

The words used for the sentences are all common ones and were selected initially from *A General Service List of English Words (West, 1965)* and then checked against a word list used in schools (Schonell, 1966). This was to ensure that the tests were suitable for use with school children as well as with adults. Adjectives (with semantic frequencies of over 100 per 5 million) and nouns and verbs (with frequencies of over 250 per 5 million) were listed and numbered in three alphabetical lists. No words of less than three or more than ten letters were used (except a few plurals of eleven letters). Longer words were not used because of possible pronunciation difficulties in reading aloud, and to help make the visual appearance of the printed lines comparable.

Sentences were then made up by picking words from the lists in the sequence adjective-noun-verb-adjective-noun. The words were chosen using random number tables (Kendall and Babington Smith, 1960), and were used once only. Six sentences were strung together to make up each test passage — 32 in all.

32

Visual appearance

Each passage was checked and corrected by word substitution within the groups for:

(a) line length – five lines of 38-41 characters and spaces per line, consecutive lines not to differ by more than 2 characters and not more than one line out of the five with only 38 characters. This was to ensure that the line lengths did not look *too* uneven, although no attempt at justified setting was made. A further check and adjustment was made at printing proof stage for line length and "rivers" (i.e. spaces between words that accidentally align, forming distracting vertical channels of white through a block of type). A maximum of 4 characters was taken as an acceptable difference between the shortest line and the longest line in each passage.

(b) only the first line of each passage to begin with a new sentence and a capital letter; the last sentence was to be incomplete. This was also to aid continuous reading from one line to another.

(c) each line to begin with a different letter, and consecutive words to begin with different letters.

(d) each line, except the last one, to have at least one descending letter, e.g. "p", and one ascending letter e.g. "b".

Ease of reading

The groups of sentences were tested with normally-sighted readers to eliminate alliteration and tongue twisting phrases, words with difficult or ambiguous pronunciations, and hidden meanings. The 32 test passages finally used are included in Appendix A.

Allocation to typographic variables

Although the typographic specification in Table 6 produce a total of 96 different combinations (2 faces × 2 weights × 6 sizes × 4 spacings), only 32 different combinations were in effect being tested (see Sections 6.2 and 6.3). Each subject read tests in either 12 and 14 point, or 14 and 16 point, or 16 and 18 point, or 18 and 20 point, or 20 and 24 point. By dividing the 32 test passages randomly into 2 groups, numbered 1-16 and 17-32, and then allocating them to alternate point sizes, it was necessary to have only 32 different passages for the total of 96 printings. Thus the two groups of test passages were used for the six type sizes as follows:

12 point . . . . test passages 1-16
14 point . . . . " " 17-32
16 point . . . . " " 1-16
18 point . . . . " " 17-32
20 point . . . . " " 1-16
24 point . . . . " " 17-32

The passages within each group of 16 were then allocated randomly to the different typographic conditions as shown in Table 7.

Table 7

ALLOCATION OF TEST PASSAGES TO TYPOGRAPHIC VARIABLES

FACE		Gill Sans 1								Plantin 2							
WEIGHT		Medium 1				Bold 2				Medium 1				Bold 2			
SPACING*		1	2	3	4	1	2	3	4	1	2	3	4	1	2	3	4
SIZE	12 point	11	16	9	6	3	1	15	14	13	10	2	5	12	7	4	8
	14 "	20	17	30	21	27	23	26	18	31	24	32	22	29	19	25	28
	16 "	15	13	4	12	8	16	6	9	2	3	5	7	1	10	11	14
	18 "	31	22	17	18	30	20	28	25	26	29	24	32	23	27	21	19
	20 "	13	9	12	3	15	2	16	11	14	7	10	8	5	1	6	4
	24 "	18	26	19	22	21	24	20	32	17	30	23	31	25	28	27	29

Key Number of Test Passage

*Spacing   1 = normal letter, 5 unit word, no leading

2 = 2 unit letter, 12 unit word, no leading

3 = normal letter, 9 unit word, no leading

4 = normal letter, 5 unit word, proportionately increased leading (see Table 6)

The key numbers used in this table identify the typographic specification; for example test 32/213/14 is

Test passage	32
Face	2 = Plantin
Weight	1 = Medium
Spacing	3 = normal letter space, extra word space, no leading
Size	14 = 14 point

6.10 Test Environment

The value of many controlled legibility experiments is often minimised by the fact that the experimental situation is too far removed from real life. Results from subjects reading with their heads in fixed frames, or reading letters and words flashed on a screen for a limited period, are difficult to apply to more normal kinds of reading. Equally, the danger of carrying out tests under completely natural conditions is that extraneous variables begin to confuse results so that reliable differences due to typography are not observed at all.

Great efforts were made in this study to achieve a "controlled informality" in carrying out the tests. A "laboratory" and "clinical" environment was avoided. It was felt that this was particularly important if natural responses were to be given by the subjects, many of whom would be elderly and infirm as well as visually handicapped. It was emphasised to each reader that the tests were not tests of intelligence or eyesight: it was the print that was being tested and not the reader.

The only pieces of apparatus used were a *reading stand* (to obviate the effect of test cards being held in a shaky hand, and to make it easier to measure the reading distance), *a portable reading lamp* (to standardise quantity and position of illumination) and a *portable tape recorder* (to record the interviews and readings).

The reader sat on an upright chair at a table on which the reading stand was positioned at a comfortable height; spectacles and/or magnifying aids were used if the reader so wished.

Reading distances were not controlled except for the initial measurement of visual acuity (see Section 6.5). Each reader was free to choose his own distance, but was asked to and in fact did, read all four test cards at the same distance.

Reading speed – each reader was to read at his natural speed.

Illumination, although an important factor in reading, has not been examined in this study for the reasons discussed in Section 3.6. For these tests, illumination was standardised at 35-45 lumens per sq. ft. (and measured with a light meter) – a level of illumination comparable to that recommended for readers with defective vision by Tinker (1965). This level incidentally, is considerably better than artificial lighting in many homes. It is hard to control illumination outside a laboratory, but the level and range maintained for the tests was adequate. Kunz and Sleight (1949) suggest that once illumination exceeds about 40 lumens per sq. ft., improvement in performance due to increased illumination is very gradual. Differences in performance therefore, due to increases or decreases in illumination between 35 and 45 lumens per sq. ft., could be assumed to have a negligible effect on performances in these tests.

6.11 Interview and Test Procedures

The interviews were recorded on tape, with the permission of the subject. Each interview took about 30 minutes and was conducted in the following sequence:

1. Brief verbal description of the purpose of the investigation

2. Screening of visual acuity

3. Completion of questionnaire, filled in by the interviewer (copy included in Appendix C)

4. Reading aloud of four test passages (reading distance recorded by interviewer)

5. For the sample of 48 children, each child was then also

   (a) tested for reading age using the Schonell Graded Word Reading Test (Schonell, 1966)

(b) asked which of the four typographic tests read, he thought the easiest and clearest to read.

It was made clear to each reader that the tests were concerned with testing the effect of different kinds of print, and not with testing the readers themselves in any way. They were told that it did not matter how fast or how slow they read, or if they made mistakes or mispronounced words.

Before any interviews were carried out, there was some doubt about the "acceptability" of the rather pecular word content of the test passages. However, an initial series of pilot interviews showed that a few words of preliminary explanation was sufficient for the passages to be read quite normally as continuous text. The explanation was given as follows — "I would like you to read four short paragraphs aloud to me. They are made up of quite ordinary words strung together in short sentences, but they have been jumbled up so that they don't make any sense". Because of the apparent ease with which they were read, it was decided that it was unnecessary to give each reader a printed practice passage: such a practice passage might have introduced the complications of transfer effects discussed in Section 6.8.

6.12 Processing and Analysis of the Data

It was decided at an early stage in planning the investigation that the statistical analysis of the test results should be done by computer. The principal justification for using computers for the comparatively small amount of data involved (336 punched cards), was that the basic statistical procedure to be used — multiple regression analysis — would be done much more efficiently. Once the program was set up, it would be cheap and quick to re-run it with a number of different sub-groups of reader performances, thus making maximum use of the data collected. (Frequently a great deal of time and effort is expended in collecting basic "raw" information, which is then not fully utilised because subsequent analysis "by hand" is so time consuming and tedious.)

The information recorded at the interviews was coded and punched on to 80 column cards. A copy of the coding sheets used is included in Appendix C. The test readings were timed, and the total times, (including hesitations and errors) to 0·1 sec., were punched on the cards: the number of correct words read was also punched as raw data. Two computer programs to analyse the data were then written for use with the University of London Atlas Computer.

One program was in MVC (Multiple Variate Counter), a programming language for analysing results of surveys. The tables and correlations of the personal data from the questionnaires produced by this program are given in Sections 7.2 and 7.3, and were used to check the representativeness of the reader sample (discussed in Sections 8.1 and 8.2), and to identify sub-groups for the multiple regression analysis of the reading performances.

A further program was written in Algol, a high-level programming language designed for scientific applications. This converted the raw data on the punched cards to a form suitable for use with a standard multiple regression program.

One advantage of using multiple regression methods was that sub-groups could be tested using the identical programs, merely using a card sorter to select cards for each particular run. The sub-groups did not, of course, contain balanced experimental designs, but multiple regression is designed to allow for such imbalance.

For the dependent variable of the regression, two different measures were tried, one based upon the number of words correctly read, the other on the time taken to read them. It was found that either measure gave a similar pattern of results, but that the latter did so more clearly, and this was therefore adopted.

Each of the 32 passages, all in the same type style, had been tested on the same sample of 10 normally-sighted people. The average time per word of these readings gave a "bogey" for each passage.

For each test, read by the partially-sighted subjects, the average time per correct word was calculated, and its ratio found to the appropriate "bogey". There was a strong positive correlation between the mean and the variability of these values, so logarithms of the values were taken to produce more nearly constant variability.

Finally the four readings for each subject were expressed as deviations about the mean value of that subject, so as largely to eliminate consistent subject differences unrelated to the factors under test. These deviations were the values eventually used as the dependent variable.

It should be noted that taking the ratio to "bogey", eliminates the units involved, and the numbers analysed are thus pure dimensionless numbers.

For the purposes of this study, this measure has been called the "reading performance".

Part III

Results

7.0 BASIC STATISTICAL RESULTS

The purpose of this research project has been to collect some reliable facts that would help printers and publishers to produce more legible books for readers with defective sight. The methods used to collect the basic data have been discussed at some length in the previous section, but it may be helpful to summarise them here before describing the results of the investigation.

Test passages were printed to illustrate differences in typography (type face, weight, size and spacing). A group of adults and another of children were then asked to read these tests aloud. Each reader was given tests in type sizes close to the lower limit of his vision, so that even small differences due to typography might be observable. The tests were carried out in such a way as to retain as many as possible of the physiological and psychological characteristics of normal reading processes. The times taken and number of errors made by each reader were then used as the basis of a statistical analysis relating reading efficiency to style of print.

As with any investigation, it can be inaccurate and misleading to apply the results to situations or conditions other than those under which the particular research was carried out. It is therefore necessary to sound a note of caution about drawing general conclusions from this study. However, equally misleading conclusions can sometimes be reached by users of research results, who are forced to make their own interpretation from bare statistics because the person responsible for the work has not interpreted the results in practical terms. In an attempt to avoid these dangers, this report deals with the results of the investigation in two ways, giving first the objective statistical results, followed by an interpretation and suggested conclusions.

(The raw data, mostly in the form of tape recordings, is too voluminous to be included in this report, but are available from the author.)

7.1 Personal Data — Adults

Personal data were collected about each reader for two main reasons:

1. The readers were volunteers and not a pre-selected sample, so that it was important to be able to check subsequently that they

were not unrepresentative of the total population.

2. The personal data were to be used to identify sub-groups of readers for the analysis of the reading performances. Were there differences in reading performances for example, between those suffering from cataract and those suffering from glaucoma, or between avid readers and those who only read the sports page of the newspaper?

But in addition to its use in the analysis of the typographic legibility tests, and therefore its relevance for printers and publishers, the information collected in the course of this investigation may be of interest for those concerned in other and more general ways with the education and welfare of the visually handicapped.

All the information was given by the readers themselves or observed by the interviewer, except for the data on eye diseases and on registration; the source of this information, which is confidential as to cases, was the official BD8 forms used for admission to the Registers of the Blind and Partially-Sighted. In the case of children, additional medical information was supplied from school records.

The basic data are summarised in the following tables: their relevance to the problems of legibility is discussed in Section 8.0.

Table 8		288 adults
SEX		
Male	33%	(94)
Female	67%	(194)
	100%	(288)
AGE		
18 - 20	2%	(6)
21 - 49	15%	(44)
50 - 64	22%	(62)
65 - 79 } 65 and over 61% {	42%	(121)
80 and over } {	19%	(55)
	100%	(288)
EDUCATION		
Left school at 14 and under	64%	(185)
" " " 15 or 16	22%	(63)
" " " 17 and over	14%	(40)
	100%	(288)
SOCIO-ECONOMIC CLASS (Census of Population Classification)		
Professional and managerial	9%	(27)
Non-manual, skilled and semi-skilled	74%	(214)
Unskilled	16%	(47)
	99%	(288)

READING HABITS

An attempt was made to assess the print reading "habits" of the adult group in terms of degree of interest and taste.

Reading Taste

Interest: described themselves as:	Newspapers only		"Low Brow"		"Middle Brow"		"High Brow"		Total	
"Serious" readers[1]	0%	(0)	0%	(0)	1%	(3)	14%	(41)	15%	(44)
"Average" readers	5%	(15)[2]	21%	(61)	34%	(97)	0%	(0)	60%	(173)
"Uninterested" readers	9%	(26)[2]	5%	(15)	1%	(2)	0%	(0)	15%	(43)
Brought up on Braille but able to read print	2%	(7)	1%	(4)	5%	(15)	1%	(2)	9%	(28)
Total	16%	(48)	27%	(80)	41%	(117)	15%	(43)	99%	(288)

[1] Sub-group 2,   [2] Sub-group 3 in reading performance analyses — see tables 23 and 24

Library Use

Belong at present time	47%	(136)
Given it up	28%	(80)
Never belonged	25%	(72)
	100%	(288)

VISION LOSS
(with spectacle correction at time of interview)

(a) Near Vision: Reduced Snellen chart at 35 cms. (14 ins.)					(b) Distance Vision: Snellen chart at 6 metres
3%	(10)	6/9 or better	(10)	3%	
6%	(16)	6/12	(16)	6%	
15%	(43)	6/18	(29)	10%	
12%	(34)	6/24	(37)	13%	
17%	(50)	6/36	(51)	18%	
17%	(50)	6/60	(56)	19%	
30%	(86)	worse	(81)	28%	
100%	(288)		(280)	97%	
				3% unknown	

Reading Vision

(c) Reading Test Types at 35 cms. (14 ins.)					(d) Reading Test Types at own reading distance, and using magnifying and low vision aids if necessary
30%	(88)	12 point type	(186)	65%	
4%	(11)	14 " "	(6)	1%	
9%	(25)	16 " "	(31)	11%	
3%	(8)	18 " "	(13)	5%	
4%	(12)	20 " "	(9)	3%	
12%	(34)	24 " "	(43)	15%	
11%	(31)	36 " "	(0)	0%	
10%	(38)	48 " "	(0)	0%	
17%	(49)	worse	(0)	0%	
100%	(288)		(288)	100%	

Table 11 | 288 Adults

USE OF VISION IN DAILY LIFE

Reading Vision: Reading test types at own distance - table 10(d)	General vision use now			Print reading now	
	Job/Housewife	Recreation	Nothing	Ordinary/ Large Print	Nothing/ Headlines only
12 point	43% (125)	20% (58)	1% (3)	36% (104)	28% (82)
14/16/18 point	10% (28)	7% (21)	0% (1)	8% (23)	9% (27)
20/24 point	11% (31)	7% (19)	1% (2)	5% (14)	13% (38)
Totals	64% (184)	34% (98)	2% (6) 100% (288)	49% (141)	50% (147) 99% (288)

Table 12 | 288 Adults

CAUSE OF VISION LOSS

34% of the adults suffered from more than one eye disease. As it is often impossible to determine the major cause of functional loss, all the diagnoses have been used in this analysis i.e. 330 amongst 241 adults. – No information was available for 47 out of the total of 288.

CAUSE BY CLINICAL ENTITY

Lens:	Cataract (incl. congenital cataract & one case of dislocated lens)	27%	(90)
Uveal Tract:	Iritis	2%	(8)
Globe:	Nystagmus	3%	(10)
	Myopic conditions	13%	(43)
	Glaucoma	13%	(42)
Cornea:	Keratitis	2%	(7)
	Corneal scarring	2%	(7)
Optic Nerve:	Optic Atrophy	5%	(16)
Retina:	Retinopathy	5%	(15)
	Detachment	3%	(11)
	Macular Degeneration	11%	(36)
Others (each less than 2%)		14%	(45)
		100%	(330)

OCCURRENCE OF MOST COMMON DISEASES
(at least 4 cases)

35 different diseases occurred amongst the 241 adults for whom diagnoses were available, but some of the conditions were much more common than others. 67% (162) of the adults suffered from only 8 diseases, either as a sole cause or in combination, as follows:

Single Causes		Multiple Causes	
Cataract	36 adults[1]	Cataract & Glaucoma	15 adults
Macular Degeneration	23 " [2]	Cataract & Myopia	8 "
Myopia	19 " [3]	Cataract & Macular Degeneration	7 "
Glaucoma	19 " [4]	Cataract & Retinopathy	6 "
Optic Atrophy	13 "		
Retinopathy	7 "		
Corneal Scarring	5 "		
Detached Retina	4 "		

[1] Sub-group 4, [2] Sub-group 5, [3] Sub-group 6, [4] Sub-group 7 in reading performance analyses – see tables 23 and 24.

N.B. Some of these 8 diseases occurred combined with some of the less common ones, but such cases are not included here.

Table 13

READING DISTANCES

Screenings of Distance and Near Vision were carried out at standard distances of 6 metres and 35cms. (14ins.) respectively, but for reading the subsequent test printings, each reader was allowed to choose his own "natural" distance.

"Natural" reading distance and Near Vision (reduced Snellen) at 35cms.

	better than 6/24		6/24		6/36		worse than 6/36	
less than 4"	0%	(0)	0%	(0)	0%	(0)	20%	(27)
4 – 7"	0%	(0)	12%	(4)	32%	(16)	55%	(74)
8 – 11"	22%	(15)	56%	(19)	30%	(15)	21%	(29)
12 – 15" (approx. average for normal sight)	41%	(28)	26%	(9)	26%	(13)	4%	(5)
more than 15"	38%	(26)	6%	(2)	12%	(6)	0%	(0)
	101%	(69)	100%	(34)	100%	(50)	100%	(135)

"Natural" reading distance and Reading Test Types at own distance

	12 point type		14/16/18/20 point type		24 point type	
less than 4"	7%	(14)	5%	(3)	23%	(10)
4 – 7"	28%	(52)	44%	(26)	37%	(16)
8 – 11"	28%	(51)	27%	(16)	26%	(11)
12 – 15"	22%	(41)	17%	(10)	9%	(4)
more than 15"	15%	(28)	7%	(4)	5%	(2)
	100%	(186)	100%	(59)	100%	(43)

Reading distance and disease

	Cataract only		Macular Deg. only		Myopia only		Glaucoma only	
less than 8"	31%	(11)	49%	(11)	68%	(13)	36%	(7)
8 – 15"	47%	(17)	51%	(12)	32%	(6)	58%	(11)
more than 15"	22%	(8)	0%	(0)	0%	(0)	5%	(1)
	100%	(36)	100%	(23)	100%	(19)	99%	(19)

Table 14   288 Adults

DURATION OF VISION LOSS

Affected since birth/early childhood	25%	(72)[1]
Affected during training/first job	3%	(10)
Affected 20-50 years old	15%	(45)
Affected after 50 years old (giving up job using near vision)	11%	(33)
Affected after 50 years old (giving up other type of job)	40%	(112)[2]
Uncertain	6%	(16)
	100%	(288)

[1] Sub-group 10 and [2] Sub-group 11 in reading performance analyses –
see tables 23 and 24

Table 15   288 Adults

USE OF OPTICAL AIDS

Aids used for tests

Spectacles		63%	(181)
Spectacles & magnifier	Aids – 74%	2%	(6)
Magnifier only		2%	(6)
Low Vision Aids		7%	(19)
Broken or forgotten	None – 26%	6%	(17)
No aids		20%	(59)
		100%	288

Aids used in daily life

Spectacles for close work only	4%	(12)
Spectacles for distance only	8%	(24)
Spectacles all the time	32%	(91)
Magnifier with/without spectacles for close work	40%	(114)
Low Vision Aid occasionally/for all close work	12%	(33)
No optical aids used	5%	(14)
	100%	(288)

95% using some kind of aid at least some of the time

Table 16   288 Adults

REGISTRATION AND VISION

	Blind Register	Partially-Sighted Register*	not known	not registered
Distance Vision				
6/9 or better	1	1	0	8
6/12	1	8	7	0
6/18	5	16	6	2
6/24	7	25	4	1
6/36	4	36	8	3
6/60	20	26	8	2
worse	51	17	9	4
not known	1	4	2	1
	90	133	44	21
	31%	46%	15%	7%

Totals
288
99%

* including 13 uncertain whether on Blind or Partially-Sighted Register.

43

7.2 Personal Data – Children

A number of the questions put to the adult readers were not applicable
to the children: also replies to questions about reading habits were
found to be unsatisfactory. Only those children with a reading age
of at least 11, assessed by the Schonell Graded Word Reading Test
(Schonell, 1966), were included in the sample.

Table 17 [48 children]

SEX

Male	52%	(25)
Female	48%	(23)
	100%	48

AGE

Chronological Age – under 14 (but over 8)	29%	(14)
14 - 17	71%	(34)
	100%	48

Reading Age	–	11 - 12½	40%	(19)
		over 12½	60%	(29)
			100%	48

EDUCATION

All 48 children were at special schools for the Partially-Sighted,
using normal school text books for at least some of their work.

Table 18 [48 children]

VISION LOSS
(with spectacle correction at time of interview)

	2%	(1)	6/9 or better	(2)	4%
	17%	(8)	6/12	(7)	15%
(a)	21%	(10)	6/18	(9)	19%
Near Vision: Reduced	8%	(4)	6/24	(5)	10%
Snellen chart at	23%	(11)	6/36	(5)	10%
35 cms. (14 ins.)	10%	(5)	6/60	(16)	33%
	19%	(9)	worse	(4)	8%
	100%	(48)		(48)	99%

(b) *Distance Vision:* Snellen chart at 6 metres

Reading Vision

	46%	(22)	12 point type	(47)	98%
	0%	(0)	14 " "	(0)	0%
	8%	(4)	16 " "	(1)	2%
(c)	2%	(1)	18 " "	(0)	0%
Reading Test Types	6%	(3)	20 " "	(0)	0%
at 35 cms. (14 ins.)	19%	(9)	24 " "	(0)	0%
	11%	(5)	36 " "	(0)	0%
	2%	(1)	48 " "	(0)	0%
	6%	(3)	worse	(0)	0%
	100%	(48)		(48)	100%

(d) Reading Test Types at own reading distance, and using magnifying and low vision aids if necessary

Table 19   48 children

CAUSE OF VISION LOSS

54% of the 48 children suffered from more than one eye disease. As it is often difficult to determine the major cause of functional loss, all the diagnoses have been used in this analysis, i.e. 81 amongst the 48 children.

CAUSE BY CLINICAL ENTITY

Lens:	Cataract (incl. 1 case of dislocated lens)	9%	(7)
Globe:	Coloboma	2%	(2)
	Aniridia	2%	(2)
	Microphthalmos	2%	(2)
	Albinism	9%	(7)
	Nystagmus	31%	(25)
	Myopia	23%	(19)
Optic Nerve:	Optic Atrophy	9%	(7)
Retina:	Retrolental Fibroplasia	4%	(3)
Others (each less than 2%)		9%	(7)
		100%	(81)

OCCURRENCE OF PARTICULAR DISEASES

16 different diseases occurred amongst the 48 children

Single Causes

Myopia	9 children
Cataract	4 "
Nystagmus	4 "
Optic Atrophy	1 "
Macular Degeneration	1 "
Detached Retina	1 "
Marfans Syndrome (dislocated lens)	1 "
Hydrophthalmos	1 "

Multiple Causes

Nystagmus and Albinism	4 "
" " Myopia	3 "
" " Optic Atrophy	3 "
" " Coloboma	2 "
" " Cataract	1 "
" " Aniridia	1 "
Nystagmus, Myopia and Aniridia	2 "
" " " Albinism	1 "
" " " Optic Atrophy	1 "
" " " Retrolental Fibroplasia	1 "
" Albinism and Macular Aplasia	1 "
" Optic Atrophy & Retrolental Fibroplasia	1 "
Myopia and Retrolental Fibroplasia	1 "
" " Optic Atrophy	1 "
Microphthalmos and cataract	1 "
" " aphakia	1 "
Vitreous haemorrhage and retino schisis	1 "
	48 children

21 children with more than 1 cause of blindness suffered from Nystagmus
10 "   "   "   " "   "   "   "   "   Myopia
 6 "   "   "   " "   "   "   "   "   Albinism (combined with Nystagmus in each case)
 6 "   "   "   " "   "   "   "   "   Optic Atrophy.

45

Table 20 | 48 Children |

READING DISTANCES

Screenings of Distance and Near Vision were carried out at standard distances of 6 metres and 35cms. (14ins.) respectively, but for reading the subsequent test printings, each reader was allowed to choose his own "natural" distance.

"Natural" reading distance and Near Vision (reduced Snellen) at 35 cms.

	better than 6/24		6/24		6/36		worse than 6/36	
less than 4"	0%	(0)	0%	(0)	0%	(0)	29%	(4)
4 - 7"	5%	(1)	0%	(0)	73%	(8)	71%	(10)
8 - 11"	37%	(7)	100%	(4)	18%	(2)	0%	(0)
12 - 15" (approx. average for normal sight)	42%	(8)	0%	(0)	9%	(1)	0%	(0)
more than 15"	16%	(3)	0%	(0)	0%	(0)	0%	(0)
	100%	(19)	100%	(4)	100%	(11)	100%	(14)

"Natural" reading distance and Reading Test Types at own distance

	12 point type		16 point type
less than 4"	9%	(4)	(0)
4 - 7"	38%	(18)	(1)
8 - 11"	28%	(13)	(0)
12 - 15"	19%	(9)	(0)
more than 15"	7%	(3)	(0)
	101%	(47)	(1)

Reading distances and disease

The small sample and the wide variety of diseases make a detailed analysis of reading distances statistically meaningless: only the 25 diagnoses of nystagmus and the 19 of myopia are given here, and % figures are not shown.

	Nystagmus only	Nystagmus & Albinism	Nystagmus & other causes	Myopia only	Myopia & other causes
less than 8"	1	6	9	0	6
8 - 15"	3	1	5	6	4
more than 15"	0	0	0	3	0

Table 21			48 Children	

USE OF OPTICAL AIDS

Aids used for tests

Spectacles	}		60%	(29)
Low Vision Aid	} Aids – 62% {		2%	(1)
Broken or forgotten	}		4%	(2)
No aids	} None – 37% {		33%	(16)
			99%	(48)

Aids used in daily life

Spectacles for distance only	10%	(5)
Spectacles all the time	38%	(18)
Magnifier with/without spectacles	35%	(17)
Low Vision Aid occasionally/for all close work	6%	(3)
No optical aids used	10%	(5)
	99%	48

7.3 Effect of Typography on Reading Performance — Adults and Children

The test readings were initially measured in terms of time taken and errors made. These criteria were used as the basis of the regression analysis calculations, which measured legibility in terms of "reading performances" (see Section 6.12).

The results reported as statistically significant are all beyond the 5% level i.e. $P < 0.05$, which means that there would be, in each case, less than one chance in 20 of observing such results if no real effects were operating. (This level of significance is the conventionally accepted level for experimental results of this kind). Because the number of observations within the sub-groups varied, the limits of confidence of the significant results varied (see table 23).

Principal findings

1. The relative legibility of the typographic factors tested is summarised in table 22 (the detailed typographic specifications have been given in table 6).

It should be noted that not all the factors were statistically significant for all the sub-groups of readers, nor were they all of equal importance, or of the same importance from one reader group to another. Table 23 shows comparable data for the total groups and the sub-groups: groups 1-11 are adult readers, and groups 12-15 are children.

However the mathematical sign (+ or -) of the regression coefficient for each statistically significant typographical variable remained the same from group to group. Thus the change in legibility was always in the same direction, e.g. a bolder type was more legible than a lighter type for all the groups where weight was a significant factor.

The interpretation of the interactions of the typographic factors is difficult but is relatively unimportant because the interactions were of little statistical significance compared with the main

```
Table 22
            RELATIVE LEGIBILITY OF TYPOGRAPHIC FACTORS

MAIN EFFECTS
    Size*
        Larger                                          more legible
        Smaller                                         less legible

    Weight
        Bold                                            more legible
        Medium                                          less legible

    Face
        Gill (sans serif)                               more legible
        Plantin (serif)                                 less legible

    Spacing
        Close set                                       most legible
        Extra leading                                   more legible
        Extra word spacing                              less legible
        Extra letter and word spacing                   least legible

*Each reader read two sizes – 12 & 14pt, or 14 & 16pt, or 16 & 18pt, or 18 & 20pt,
                or 20 & 24pt – according to his reading acuity

INTERACTIONS

    Size/Weight
        Smaller Bold or Larger Medium                   increase
        Larger Bold or Smaller Medium                   decrease

    Face/Weight
        Plantin Medium or Gill Bold                     increase
        Gill Medium or Plantin Bold                     decrease

Other combinations of factors were analysed – Face/Size, Face/Space, Size/Space,
                Weight/Space – but were not found to be significant
```

effects. Where an interaction does exist, it means that the joint effect of changing two variables at once, is not merely what would have been expected if the two main effects were acting independently. Thus for example, Larger size has been found more legible than Smaller, and Bold weight more legible than Medium: if the two changes are combined, however, the Smaller Bold or Larger Medium styles are found to be rather better than would be expected solely from the main effects, while the other two styles (Larger Bold and Smaller Medium) do rather worse than expected.

2. For the total adult readers (Group 1 in table 23), size, weight and face of type were all found to be statistically significant, but not equally important in their effect on legibility.

An increase in size of print achieved an improvement in reading performance of 16%: an increase in weight achieved 9% improvement (although these two factors interacted to the extent that an increase in size of a light type improved reading performance more than the same size increase of a bold type): a change from a serif face (Plantin) to a sans serif face (Gill Sans) improved reading performances by 4%. The total effect of changing from the worst to the best type was an improvement of 35%.

3. For the total group of children (Group 12 in table 23), size of type was the only typographic factor found to be statistically significant: there was a 5% improvement in reading performance with increase in size.

4. There was more variability, from test to test, in the adult's reading performances than the children's. The figures of standard deviations in table 24 show this e.g. ·23 for the Total Adult Group, compared with ·12 for the Total Children.

5. Also a higher proportion of that variability can be explained by the typographic changes with the adults' than with the children. The figures for % of variance in table 24 show this e.g. 15% for the adults and only 5% for the children.

6. The Personal Data available for each reader was used to identify sub-groups within the main groups, to see if any known *non*-typographic variables were of importance.

The sub-groups for which there were statistically significant results are listed in table 23: it should be noted that they were not necessarily mutually exclusive. The standard deviations and % of variance due to typography in Table 24 show further differences between the sub-groups.

7. Table 23 shows that the actual amount of change in performance due to the typographic variables being tested, differed from group to group, and from one typographic factor to another.

8. After they had read the tests, the children (but not the adults) were asked which of the samples they had read they thought the clearest. Each child had read 4 different kinds of print so that there was a 1 in 4 chance of his subjective choice coinciding with his best performance. In fact, out of the 48 children only 12 (i.e. 1 in 4 precisely) chose the type with which they had performed best. Thus there was no correlation between personal subjective judgment and objective reading performance. There was also no consistency in type preference from child to child.

9. On the basis of the regression analysis, a 35% improvement in the reading performance of the adult group was predicted for a change from the least favourable to the most favourable combinations of type size, weight, face and spacing. The performances of the nine readers in the sample who had read both the best and the worst print combinations, were subsequently analysed: it was found that the average improvement had in fact been 34%, thus supporting the statistical predictions.

Table 23

EFFECT OF TYPOGRAPHIC CHANGES ON READING PERFORMANCE

READER GROUP[1]	TYPOGRAPHIC FACTORS						
	Size	Weight	Face	Space	Size/ Weight	Face/ Weight	Total
1. TOTAL ADULTS	*** 16% (14-19%)	*** 9% (6-12%)	** 4% (1-7%)	ns	* 3% (0-5%)	ns	35% (22-50%)
Reading Interest[2] — 2. Serious	*** 16% (10-23%)	ns	ns	* 3% (0-5%)	ns	ns	20% (10-29%)
3. Newspapers only	*** 15% (5-24%)	*** 8% (1-16%)	ns	ns	ns	ns	24% (6-44%)
Cause of Vision[3] Loss — 4. Cataract	ns	** 7% (2-13%)	ns	ns	** 10% (4-16%)	ns	18% (6-31%)
5. Macular Degeneration	* 11% (2-20%)	ns	* 10% (1-19%)	ns	ns	ns	22% (3-43%)
6. Myopia	** 17% (6-29%)	ns	ns	ns	ns	ns	17% (6-29%)
7. Glaucoma	*** 22% (11-34%)	** 18% (7-30%)	ns	ns	ns	ns	44% (19-74%)
Reading Vision — 8. Smallest Test Size	*** 14% (9-20%)	* 5% (0-11%)	** 7% (1-12%)	ns	* 5% (0-11%)	ns	35% (10-66%)
9. Largest Test Size[5]	*** 40% (24-58%)	** 23% (10-39%)	ns	ns	ns	ns	72% (36-120%)
Duration of Vision Defect[6] — 10. Since birth	*** 16% (11-21%)	** 6% (1-11%)	ns	ns	ns	* 6% (1-10%)	30% (13-48%)
11. After age of 50	*** 16% (12-21%)	*** 12% (8-17%)	** 7% (3-11%)	ns	ns	ns	36% (25-57%)
12. TOTAL CHILDREN	** 5% (2-9%)	ns	ns	ns	ns	ns	5% (2-9%)
Reading Distance — 13. Less than 8ins.[7]	*** 10% (4-16%)	ns	ns	ns	ns	ns	10% (4-16%)
14. 8 ins. or more[8]	ns	* 5% (1-10%)	ns	ns	ns	ns	5% (1-10%)
15. Test size within visual limits	ns	* 8% (1-14%)	ns	ns	* 7% (1-14%)	ns	16% (2-30%)

Statistical Significance
*** very highly significant (P < 0·001)
** highly significant (P < 0·01)
* significant (P < 0·05)
ns not significant

Confidence limits on the point estimates of % change in legibility, vary between the groups because of the different numbers of observations in each; these limits are given in brackets after the point estimates. The numbers of observations in each group are shown in table 24.

Table 24

STATISTICAL CRITERIA

Reader Group[1]		Number of observations (4 per subject)	Standard Deviation	% variance attributable to typography
1. Total Adults		1152	·23	15%
Reading Interest[2]	2. Serious	176	·20	16%
	3. Newspapers only	160	·23	13%
Cause of Defect[3]	4. Cataract	144	·17	10%
	5. Macular Degeneration	92	·21	10%
	6. Myopia	76	·23	11%
	7. Glaucoma	76	·24	21%
Reading Vision	8. Smallest Test Size[4]	204	·20	13%
	9. Largest Test Size[5]	76	·32	29%
Duration[6] of Vision Defect	10. Since birth	288	·20	15%
	11. After age of 50	448	·23	17%
12. Total Children		192	·12	5%
Reading Distance	13. Less than 8 inches.[7]	84	·13	12%
	14. 8 inches or more.[8]	100	·11	5%
	15. Test size within visual limits	76	·14	10%

Footnotes to Tables 23 and 24

[1] The sub-groups are not all mutually exclusive, although groups within each sub-group are e.g. a "Serious" reader might also have "Cataract", but a reader with "Glaucoma" did not also have "Macular Degeneration".

[2] See table 9.

[3] See table 12.

[4] Those able to read the smallest test sizes (12/14 point), using no magnifying aids and at a close reading distance of less than 8".

[5] Those able to read only the largest test sizes (20/24 point), using no magnifying aids and at a close reading distance of less than 8".

[6] See table 14.

[7] Those reading tests using no magnifying aids and at a close reading distance of less than 8".

[8] Those reading tests using no magnifying aids but at a reading distance of 8" or more.

8.0 COMMENT

The difficulties of drawing general conclusions from particular results have been mentioned at the beginning of the last section. Assuming the statistical reliability of the results (see Section 7.3), the main dangers are related to

(a) the representativeness of the sample population,

(b) the validity of applying results from testing particular typographic variables under particular experimental reading conditions, to similar but untested typographic and reading situations.

8.1 Representativeness of Sample

288 adults were interviewed for the investigation and it has been estimated earlier in this report that there may be 100,000 people in England and Wales who are partially-sighted but who can still see some print: thus the sample size used is only a small proportion of the total number. But the worth of the results from a sample depends almost solely on the number in the sample and the degree of its representativeness, and hardly at all on the proportion of the population that it represents. It was therefore important to establish the representativeness of the sample.

Other statistical sources have provided a cross check for some of the personal characteristics of the Reader Sample interviewed in this investigation. Tables 25, 26 and 27 show the comparative figures that are available for adults.

From a comparison between the figures for the Reader Sample (on the left of each table) and those collected from a variety of different official sources (and shown on the right of the tables), it is reasonable to conclude that the sample was not unduly biased.

The *Age* and *Sex* characteristics of the Sample (table 25) are not comparable with the Total Population, but do compare well with the Blind and Partially-Sighted population. As discussed earlier in this report, there is a high incidence of visual defects in the older age groups which would account for the disparity in relation to the Total Population.

The comparable statistics given for *Education* and *Socio-economic class* (table 25) show that the Sample was reasonably representative of the total normally sighted population, although the proportion of the Professional and Managerial class was a little low, perhaps because most of the readers were contacted through welfare clubs and services: the disproportion may also reflect the older age distribution of the Sample.

52

Table 25　　　　　　　　　　　　　　　　　　　　　　　　　　　　　Adults

COMPARISON OF READER SAMPLE & TOTAL POPULATION

Reader Sample 1967		Total Population 1961 Census	Partially Sighted Register* 1967	Blind Register* 1967
	SEX	(England and Wales, aged 18 and over)		
33%	Male	48%	37%	39%
67%	Female	52%	63%	61%
100%		100%	100%	100%
	AGE			
17%†	21 - 49	57%	15%	11%
22%	50 - 64	27%	14%	17%
61%	65 and over	16%	71%	72%
100%		100%	100%	100%
	EDUCATION			
64%	Left school at at 14 and under	60%		
22%	at 15 or 16	31%		
14%	at 17 and over	9%		
100%		100%		
	SOCIO-ECONOMIC CLASS		Comparable statistics not available	
9%	Professional and Managerial	14%		
74%	Non-manual, skilled and semi-skilled	74%		
16%	Unskilled	8%		
0%	Others	4%		
99%		100%		

† includes 2% aged 18-20　　　　　　　　　　* Ministry of Health, 1968

The statistics given for *Cause of Vision Loss* (table 26) are difficult to use for comparison. The disparities in the official statistics are because the 1965 figures do not include people over 65, and therefore exclude many cases of "old age" defects: this largely explains the difference in the figures for lens (principally senile cataract) and retinal defects (particularly macular degeneration). But it does seem that the Reader Sample contained too few cases of diseases of the uveal tract and retina, and too many cases of diseases of the globe (principally myopia) and miscellaneous causes. All the same the Sample was not seriously biased by the absence or inclusion of any particularly common or uncommon disease.

Table 26   Adults

COMPARISON OF READER SAMPLE & TOTAL POPULATION
CAUSE OF VISION LOSS

Reader Sample 1967		Blindness* 1955-60	Blindness† 1965	Partial Sight† 1965
27%	Lens	24%	12%	17%
2%	Uveal Tract	11%	18%	20%
29%	Globe	16%	14%	18%
4%	Cornea	2%	3%	5%
5%	Optic Nerve	5%	15%	10%
19%	Retina	41%	36%	27%
14%	Others	1%	2%	3%
100%		100%	100%	100%

     * new Blind Registrations – all ages (Ministry of Health, 1966)

     † new Registrations – less than 65 years old (Ministry of Health, 1967)

Table 27   Adults

COMPARISON OF READER SAMPLE & TOTAL POPULATION
DURATION OF VISION LOSS

Reader Sample 1967		Blind Register* 1967
25%	Affected since birth/early childhood	15%
3%	Affected during training/first job	2%
15%	Affected 20-50	16%
51%	Affected after 50	66%
6%	Uncertain	1%
100%		100%

     * Ministry of Health, 1968

The figures for *Duration of Vision Loss* (table 27), also suggest that the Sample was not unduly biased. It did contain rather too few people whose sight deteriorated after the age of 50, and this was probably because those in the older age groups are less mobile and/or suffering from deafness, and therefore less likely to volunteer for interview. Unfortunately no figures were available for comparing the *amount* of vision loss.

Fewer children were interviewed than adults – only 48. It had been decided early on in the project that the main emphasis should be on a study of adult needs (see Section 4.4): the tests with children were therefore subsidiary to the principal tests with the 288 adults, and a smaller group of 48 was considered adequate.

Tables 28 and 29 show comparable statistics for the sample of children interviewed and the total population.

Table 28   [Children]

COMPARISON OF READER SAMPLE & TOTAL POPULATION

Reader Sample: 1967 (aged 8-17, with reading age over 11)	SEX	Total Population 1961 Census (aged 10-14)	Partially Sighted Register* 1967 (aged 11-15) England and Wales	Special School Survey†
52%	Male	51%	62%	66%
48%	Female	49%	38%	44%
100%		100%	100%	100%

     * Ministry of Health, 1968   † Dept. of Education and Science, 1968

Table 29   [Children]

COMPARISON OF READER SAMPLE & TOTAL POPULATION
VISION LOSS

Reader Sample 1967	DISTANCE VISION	Special School Survey†
38%	6/18 or better	22%
20%	6/24 - 6/36	35%
41%	6/60 or worse	42%
0%	unknown	1%
99%		100%

Reader Sample* 1967	CAUSE	Special School Survey† born 1951-55
9%	Lens: Cataract	27%
9%	Globe: Albinism	10%
31%	Nystagmus	11%
23%	Myopia	14%
9%	Optic Nerve: Atrophy	12%
4%	Retina: Retrolental Fibroplasia	6%
15%	Others (each less than 2%)	20%
100%		100%

     * 94% of the Sample was born 1951-55   † Dept. Education and Science, 1968

Comparison of the Reader Sample of children with the other statistical sources show some discrepancies. For *Sex*, the Sample compared more exactly with the total normally-sighted population than with the partially-sighted one. No comparable figures were available for near visual acuity, but figures for *Distance Vision* suggest that the Sample contained rather too many children with vision of 6/18 or better and rather too few with vision of 6/24 or 6/36: however, the proportion of those with vision of 6/60 or worse was very representative of the total population in partially-sighted schools. Comparison of *Cause of Vision Loss* shows discrepancies in relation to the incidence of cataract, nystagmus and myopia. However in the case of nystagmus the Reader Sample includes all cases, whereas the Special School Survey only includes those cases where nystagmus was the only known cause. The discrepancy between Cataract and Myopia is less easy to explain. One possible reason is related to intelligence and reading ability. There is some evidence that children with cataract have lower I.Q.'s than those with myopia (Dept. Education & Science, 1968). The principal criteria for inclusion in the Sample was a reading age of at least 11 years, so this may be a cause of the bias.

In conclusion it is reasonable to say that the Sample of children interviewed and tested in this investigation are representative of the older, brighter children in schools for the partially-sighted, i.e. results may apply only to children over the age of 9 or 10 and with a reading age of at least 11.

8.2   Validity of Results

The detailed experimental results reported in Section 7.0 are all beyond the 5% level of significance, i.e. there would be, in each case, less than one chance in twenty of observing such a result if there were no real effects operating. It therefore seems likely that the typographic differences tested have indeed caused the performance differences. Comparison between the Reader Sample tested and the total population has shown that the sample that carried out the tests was reasonably representative of the total partially-sighted population. It is therefore reasonable to suggest that the results of the investigation are valid for the total partially-sighted population.

But can the results be applied to other reading situations? Section 6.0 includes a discussion of the methodological problems involved. The tests, although short and made up of random sentences, were designed to simulate the normal reading of continuous prose. This method of measuring legibility has not been fully validated, but it seems subjectively reasonable. The readers *sounded* as if they were reading normally, despite the "nonsense" sentences, which suggests that normal physiological and psychological reading mechanisms were being used. It might be argued that the brevity of the test passages could invalidate results. But Tinker (1963), in evaluating methods in legibility research for the normally-sighted, states that differences found for periods as short as 1 minute, hold or increase slightly for longer work periods. Some of the tests in the present investigation were read in less than a minute, but the readers were reading at or near their visual limit (as all visually handicapped readers have to), and so differences are likely to be measurable over a shorter test period than is necessary for normally sighted readers. It also seems reasonable to suggest that differences observed with partially-sighted readers are particularly likely to increase, rather than decrease, over longer reading periods. Of course this is not to say that differences *not* observed during these tests would not appear under different situations, but merely that the differences for the short passages will almost certainly be important in more extended reading, even if other factors come into play then as well. A final point encouraging belief in the validity of the methods used, is that some of the results confirmed differences that would be expected on common sense grounds anyway, for example, the relative importance of *size* of print.

8.3 Conclusions

Can these results then be the basis for any general conclusions about designing legible print for partial-sight? Some generalisations about typographic and other factors affecting text reading for partially-sighted readers are certainly suggested by the investigation.

Type Size

This investigation has shown that size is one of the most important factors for partially-sighted readers. But this is not to say that books in extra-large print are required by all partially-sighted readers, or that legibility increases indefinitely with successive increases in size of print. Some further explanation of this paradox is necessary before discussing the importance of other typographic factors for partial-sight.

The starting point for explaining the effect of changes in print size is the normal eye. The lens of the eye can be altered in shape by the ciliary muscles so that any object, regardless of distance, can be focussed sharply on the retina at the back of the eye. The size of the image on the retina is related to the distance of the object from the eye, and not on its actual size. The diagrams below show the effect on image size of changing the viewing distance of the same object.

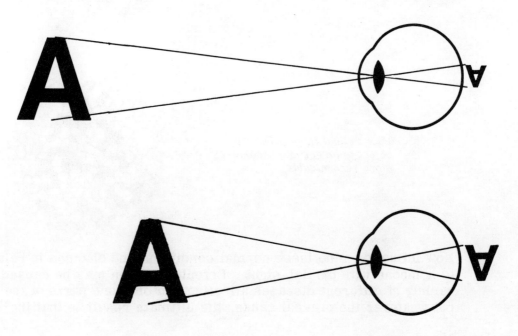

When the ciliary muscle in the normal eye is relaxed, the objects that are then in focus are those in the distance. In a child's eye, the ciliary muscle is so active that it can focus on very close objects with great ease and without doing any harm. (This is the process of accommodation). With increasing age the power of accommodation gradually gets less, culminating in presbyopia (generally at about the age of 45) when the eye is no longer able to focus clearly on very near objects.

To get round the problem of an out-of-focus image, the adult begins to have to hold the object – book or whatever – further away from his eye, thereby retaining the sharpness but decreasing the size of the image. For the normal eye the use of reading glasses compensates for the lack of focussing power in the eye, and makes it possible for the print to be held close enough to retain a good image size as well as a sharply focussed one.

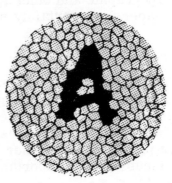

*Good retinal image
of a small object*

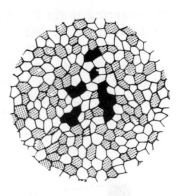

*Poor retinal image of
the same small object*

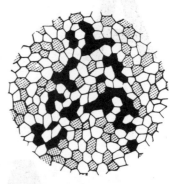

*Poor retinal image, but the
object is larger and becomes
more recognisable*

Now let us examine these normal conditions and changes in relation to someone with partial-sight. Defective vision may be caused by a variety of different diseases affecting one or more parts of the eye, but whatever the clinical cause, the ultimate result is that the image received by the retina is inadequate for the brain to perceive and "read". This inadequate retinal image may be blurred or distorted, completely or partly missing. If this image is now enlarged by some means, it may still be blurred or distorted, but there may be enough of it reaching the retina for interpretation and recognition to take place. The diagrams opposite show how a larger image can become recognisable despite blind patches in a vision field. The problem therefore is how to enlarge the image.

This study has shown very clearly that there is a basic difference between the partially-sighted adult and the partially-sighted child in coping with the problem. Because a partially-sighted child retains his powers of accommodation, even though he has one or more eye diseases, he is able to enlarge the image for himself by bringing the object close to his eyes (75% of the children interviewed read at 11 inches or less): the object is still sharply focussed, although bits of it may be missing or it may be distorted in other ways. This technique can be very successful: virtually all the children interviewed, despite the fact that they were being educated in special schools for the partially-sighted (61% of them had a distance vision of 6/36 or worse), were able to see normal 12 point print when they were not restricted to the normal reading distance of about 14 inches.

In contrast to children, partially-sighted adults are in a much more difficult position. They are, or are becoming, presbyopic as part of the normal process of growing older, and are more or less unable to achieve an enlarged and sharply focussed image by bringing the object closer. At the same time because they are partially-sighted, they have special need of a larger image. The present investigation has shown that despite the problems of presbyopia (and normal reading glasses can overcome the presbyopia even though they cannot help the principal pathological condition), partially-sighted adults do read at a closer than average distance – 69% of the adults interviewed read at 11" or less. At these close distances the image although larger, will not be in focus for many adults and may still not be large enough to be recognised. There is evidence for this in the fact that, whereas all the children could read 12 point print if it was close enough, only 65% of the adult sample could read this size.

These facts suggest that partially-sighted adults often do need larger-than-average print (i.e. larger than 10-12 point) but that children can achieve adequate enlargement naturally by merely bringing normal print close to their eyes. But what is "adequate" enlargement – can legibility for children and adults go on being increased by yet further enlargement? The results of this investigation suggest that "extra" enlargement does not continue to increase legibility. Comparable tests were not carried out with the adult readers, but the children who read the tests at a distance of 8" or more were not affected by size changes. All but two of these 25 children had a distance acuity better than 6/36 and it may be inferred that they were reading test sizes well within their visual limits. This conclusion is supported by results from the children who were specifically given test sizes within their visual limits, although for these children, a larger size did help the disadvantages of a less bold type. It would seem therefore that for children at least, continuing enlargement ceases to bring the benefit of increased legibility. This evidence supports accepted ideas about the general mechanics of reading and the role of eye movements in normal reading. The eye scans text in a series of stops and starts, and "reading" takes place during the stops (or fixations): during each fixation the eye takes in the words on either side of the most clearly focussed central point. If the print is large, fewer words or letters can be seen at a single fixation. Obviously the print must be big enough to be seen, but once it is, reading efficiency is likely to be decreased by further enlargement – each fixation will pick up less information, and there will have to be more eye movements to do the same amount of work.

A further point against over enlargement is the economic one – larger print means bigger and more expensive books. But an equally important problem may be "user resistance": bigger books may be heavy and awkward to carry to and from a library and to hold when reading, and some readers, especially children, may be self conscious and reluctant to read "different looking" books.

Type Weight

The results of the investigation show that although of secondary importance compared with size, weight (or boldness) of type does affect legibility. An increase in weight of type improves legibility for certain groups of readers. Glaucoma patients in particular are helped by the use of a bolder type, and the results also suggest that people who are not really keen readers find a bolder type more legible. The tests showed that the weight of type was more important than size, for children reading sizes within their visual capacities.

One reason for the help given by increased weight of type is probably that it is somewhat comparable with increasing size: there is more to be seen because the strokes of the letters are thicker than with a lighter type, even though the size as measured by height may be the same. If there is more of it, there is a greater chance of a recognisable image being received by the retina, although this cannot be extrapolated too far.

Boldness also, and perhaps not surprisingly, draws attention to itself, helping readers who otherwise have little natural incentive or inclination to read.

The results with children indicate that although size is the most significant factor at or near the threshold of vision, once above that lower limit, weight becomes the most important factor.

The effect of increased weight of type is important from the practical book production point of view because the use of bolder type does not incur all of the disadvantages of using a larger size of type.

Type Face

This investigation shows that differences in type faces seem to have little effect on legibility. Obviously because of odd quirks in design detail some faces are likely to be relatively illegible, and the two faces tested in this study were selected just because they did not contain such confusing idiosyncracies. However, from the typographic point of view there was a major distinction between them – one was a serif style and one was sans serif. The results show that differences in legibility between these two faces were of minor importance compared with the effect of size and weight. In the few cases when there was a significant difference, the sans serif face Gill Sans was more legible than the serif Plantin, but only for the adult readers. This is particularly interesting in view, on the one hand, of the traditionalist views that a serif face is always more legible than a sans serif, and on the other that technological developments in automatic reading and printing devices are encouraging the use of sans serif styles.

Type Spacing

An unexpected result of the investigation was to find that the spacing variations tested apparently made so little difference to legibility. There was a statistically significant but small difference observed with the sub-group of "serious" readers, who found the closest spacing most legible. This supports evidence about efficient reading that assumes rapid recognition of whole words rather than letters. The spreading out of reading units by insertion of extra space would seem to upset this process.

However two important points should be remembered in interpreting the negative results from tests of spacing. First, the tests were concerned with continuous reading – it could well be that spacing requirements for a reading task involving "search" and "selection", such as in using a dictionary, an encyclopaedia or a telephone directory, are different and that extra spacing may then become a more positive aid to legibility. Second, it must be remembered that not all the possible variations in spacing were tested (see Section 6.3). The tests indicate that extra space between the words *or* between the letters and words *or* between the lines has very little effect on legibility. It may be that legibility is only affected by altering spacing between the letters and words and lines simultaneously. Adverse comments about close spacing were quite frequently made by the readers interviewed in this study and it would seem reasonable to expect open spacing to help legibility to some extent. More work needs to be done on this point, although the present results suggest that the use of word and phrase units fundamental in normal reading, is also of importance for the partially-sighted.

Other Printing Factors

It should be remembered that, as well as the variations in spacing that have not been examined in this investigation, there are a number of other factors that may affect legibility – length of line, margins, page layout, contrast between paper and print in reflectance value and colour, and methods of reproduction. Practical and economic considerations are likely to mean that special reading material for the partially-sighted may often have to be produced from existing printed material, and there may not be the opportunity of choosing special type styles. Photographic enlargement of existing material can of course achieve an increase in type size but depending on the nature of the original material, the methods of enlargement, and the subsequent means of printing, very different results can be achieved:

enlargement of a bad original can be useless and it may be more worthwhile trying to find material which is normal size but is well printed in a bold type on good paper.

Such factors merit further investigation, particularly in order to discover their importance in relation to the basic typographic elements tested in the present study.

Illumination

The effect of illumination was not investigated in this study, but its importance is not in doubt, and has been discussed in Section 3.6.

The Partially-Sighted Readers

It is proper to conclude this report by returning to the starting point of the investigation – to the partially-sighted readers themselves. The investigation, although primarily concerned with discovering facts about print, has also collected more general information about the partially-sighted population. Some of the facts and figures presented in this report may merely confirm points already well known to those concerned with the education and welfare of the partially-sighted, others may throw a new or different light on the problems and attitudes of the partially-sighted to their handicap. Some of these findings may serve the purpose of putting specific results about typography in perspective.

The differences in typography that were tested are quite large ones from the printer's stand point and if judged aesthetically, yet some of them had little or no effect, on objective legibility. The differences in size and weight of print that did have a measureable effect still did not account for all the differences in reading performance: only some 15% of the total variance in performances of the adult readers was due to differences in typography, and only 5% in the case of the children. Typography is certainly not the only factor that affects a partially-sighted person's ability to read print.

One non-typographic factor which is of interest in relation to reading, is the cause of partial-sight. The results reported in tables 23 and 24 do suggest differences attributable to pathology. Readers with cataract were not helped by increase in size so much as increased weight of print: on the other hand readers with myopia were not helped by changes in weight, but were helped by increase in size. The group of readers with glaucoma were affected more than other groups by typographic changes, and size and weight were both important for them. Readers with macular degeneration were helped by increases in print size and a change to a sans serif type but, surprisingly, not by an increase in weight. But despite these detailed differences, the results do not present any real conflict in practical terms. In no instance was a typographic factor helpful to one group of readers, but positively bad for one of the other groups.

Another non-typographic factor which could be expected to be of the utmost importance is the amount of vision a person retains, but the results reported here show clearly that this is not a straightforward relationship. To begin with, standard clinical or laboratory measurements of visual acuity, using the Snellen notation for example,

62

can be misleading guides to a person's functional vision – that is the amount of vision he actually has available for use in everyday life. Two thirds of the adults interviewed in this investigation had a distance vision of 6/36 Snellen or worse even using spectacles, and yet over half of this group was able to see 12 point print with the help of optical aids or by bringing the print very close. In the case of the children, the discrepancy was even greater – again about two thirds of the sample had a distance vision of 6/36 Snellen or worse, yet almost all of them were able to see 12 point print. Also, what a person is physically capable of seeing may be very different from the practical use he actually makes of his remaining vision, but here again the results in this report indicate that there is no direct correlation between the two measurements. The information about the kinds of print reading actually being done at the time of the interviews is interesting in this connection. Although 64% of the adults were capable of reading 12 point print, nearly half of these said that in fact they read nothing or only the newspaper headlines. At the other end of the scale, of the people whose vision was so bad that they could see only large 20-24 point print, as many as a quarter of them still did some reading other than just headlines, although this often required use of special magnifying aids. There is a direct relationship between general interest and attitudes towards reading (usually established before any loss of vision), and how much a person actually reads after his vision deteriorates. Of the adults interviewed, a much higher proportion of "serious" than "uninterested" readers were still reading books in ordinary print, and this was not closely related to the amount of remaining vision. Clearly the personal attributes of the reader, such as will power and incentive, play as important a role as the physical amount or quality of vision, in determining how much a partially-sighted person actually reads.

However despite the relevance of these other factors, improved typography can give positive help to the partially-sighted reader. Changes in typography seem to help adult readers more than children, (although it is possible that print requirements of younger or less intelligent partially-sighted children are more critical). Increased size of print improves legibility for adults, but this is less important for most partially-sighted children, who can achieve a larger image by reading at close distances. Over-enlargement does not improve legibility and once an adequate size is reached, extra weight of print is likely to increase legibility more effectively, especially for children. The choice of type face is of relatively little importance, although results indicate that a sans-serif type may be helpful for both adults and children.

The differences in reading performance, measured in this study in terms of speed and errors, indicate that if all the best typographic features were combined, there would be an improvement of the order of 35%, compared with print using all the worst features: such improvements are worth implementing.

Summary

The investigation which is the subject of this report has been concerned with the design of reading material for the partially-sighted. Its purpose has been to collect some reliable facts that would help printers and publishers to produce more legible books for readers with defective sight. The project has not been concerned with Braille and the problems of readers unable to see even the largest print, but with people who can do some print reading but who have difficulty in seeing normal book print (10-12 point) and whose eyesight cannot be fully corrected by spectacles.

The findings reported relate to the reading of continuous printed text at close reading distances: specialised settings for tables, diagrams and reference books were not examined, nor was "reading" material in the form of road signs, labels, television displays, etc.

The typographic factors that were investigated in the objective legibility tests were type face, type weight, type size and type spacing.

Two groups of readers with defective sight co-operated in the tests — 288 adults and 48 children: all the children had a reading age of at least 11.

Statistical analysis of the reading performances, measured by time taken and mistakes made, provided data about the relative importance of the different factors tested. The results reported are statistically significant beyond the 5% level.

Sections 7·0 and 8·0 discuss the results of the investigation in detail: only the principal conclusions are set out here.

1. *Differences between adults and children*

Changes in typography affect adult readers much more than children (although print requirements for younger or less intelligent partially-sighted children may be more critical).

2. *Type Size*

Size of Type is one of the most important typographic factors for partially-sighted readers, but this is not to say that books in extra-large print are required for all partially-sighted readers, or that legibility continues to increase with successive enlargement.

There is a basic difference between adults and children in this respect. The adult often does need larger than average print, but the child, because he still retains powers of accommodation, can achieve adequate enlargement by bringing the print close to his eyes.

Enlargement much beyond the size necessary for the type to be seen, is unlikely to increase legibility.

3. *Type Weight*

Increased weight or boldness of type, although of secondary importance compared with size, also improves legibility for most partially-sighted readers. Results with children suggest that once above the lower threshold of vision, weight becomes a more important factor than size.

4. *Type Face*

The effect of differences between the type faces tested (a serif and a sans serif) is of minor importance compared with the effect of size and weight. The sans serif face was slightly more legible for the adult readers, but no measurable differences between the faces were observed with the children.

5. *Type Spacing*

Changes in spacing either between the letters and words, or between the words only, or between the lines only, do not appear to affect legibility.

6. *Cause of Partial-Sight*

Legibility does vary with typographic changes according to the pathological cause of partial-sight. However, there is no real conflict of interests here as typography that is helpful for one pathological group is not positively bad for one of the other groups.

7. *Amount of Residual Vision*

There is no direct correlation between the amount of vision remaining in a defective eye and the use a person makes of it for reading. The personal attributes of the reader — will power, incentive and interest in reading — play as important a role as the physical amount of vision in determining whether a partially-sighted person actually does much reading.

8. *Importance of Typography*

Although many other factors also affect a partially-sighted person's ability to read print easily, the part played by typography is significant, particularly for adults: the increase in legibility due to improvements in typography measured in this investigation were of the order of 35% for the adult readers.

Glossary

ACCOMMODATION – process of altering the focus of the eye by changing the curvature of the lens. To focus on close objects, the lens is made more convex by contraction of the ciliary muscle.

ALBINISM – hereditary condition of lack of pigment in skin, hair and eyes.

B.D.8 FORM – certificate of blindness and partial-sight used in the United Kingdom for admission to the Ministry of Health's Registers of Blind and of Partially Sighted Persons.

BLINDNESS – the statutory definition for purposes of registration as a blind person in the United Kingdom is "so blind as to be unable to perform any work for which eyesight is essential". In practice a person is usually considered blind if their best corrected vision is worse than 3/60 with normal field of vision, or 3/60 to 6/60 with a contracted field of vision: see Section 3.4 of this report for discussion of the problems of exact definitions.

CATARACT – opacity of the lens causing loss of visual acuity: may originate before birth (congenital) or develop progressively in the elderly (senile) or from injury (traumatic).

CONGENITAL DEFECTS – existing at birth.

CONVERGENCE – co-ordinated movement of the two eyes to allow fixation on the same near point of vision.

CORNEAL SCARRING – caused by inflammatory conditions e.g. keratitis, and resulting in loss of transparency of the cornea, and hence loss of visual acuity.

CORRECTED VISION (spectacle correction) – vision for which refractive errors, caused when the eyeball is too short (long sighted or hypermetropic) or too long (short sighted or myopic) or astigmatic (distortion due to unequal curvature of lens or cornea), are corrected by spectacles.

DISTANCE VISION – ability of the eye to see when looking at an object in the distance: 6 metres is accepted as standard for clinical measurement of distance vision.

FIELD OF VISION – the area that can be seen without movement of the eye.

FUNCTIONAL LOSS (of visual acuity) – loss of vision in relation to particular practical tasks, e.g. cooking, reading, walking about: in contrast to loss measured by objective clinical standards such as Snellen chart.

GLAUCOMA – disease caused by increase in pressure within the eye: progressive damage to the optic nerve results in loss of visual acuity.

JUSTIFICATION (in printing) – adjustment of spacing between words so that each line in a block of type is the same length, and the right side of the block as well as the left is even.

LEADING – extra space between lines of type.

LEGIBILITY – the ease and accuracy with which meaningful printed material is comprehended.

LOWER CASE – small letters e.g. a b c, in contrast to capitals.

LUMEN – unit for measuring amount of illumination: one lumen per sq.ft. is equivalent to one foot candle – that is the light given by one candle at a distance of one foot.

MACULA – central spot on the retina containing the fovea, where vision is most acute.

MACULAR DEGENERATION — disease most common in the elderly, resulting in deterioration of the central vision i.e. the area of vision used for fine detail: peripheral vision is unaffected.

MYOPIA (Myopic) — short sight i.e. the eye is too long from back to front for the light from a distance to focus naturally on the retina: it is usually corrected by spectacles but extreme myopia can be pathological, causing gradual loss of acuity resulting in blindness.

NEAR VISION — ability of the eye to see when focussed on a close object: 35 cms. (approx. 14") is accepted as standard for clinical measurement of near vision.

NYSTAGMUS — an involuntary rapid oscillatory movement of the eyeball, often congenital. It may be present in eyes which otherwise appear to be normal, but also occurs in cases of albinism and congenital cataract and retinal disorders.

OPTIC ATROPHY — degeneration of the optic nerve i.e. the channel of communication between the eye and the visual centres of the brain.

PARTIAL-SIGHT (visual handicap, defective vision) — there is no statutory definition of partial sight in the United Kingdom: for registration purposes, a person is usually considered partially-sighted if their best corrected vision is 3/60 to 6/60 with normal field of vision, or up to 6/24 with moderate contraction of the field or opacities, or 6/18 and better if there is a gross field defect.

For the purposes of this report a partially-sighted person is defined as one who because of defective eyesight, has difficulty in reading normal size book print (10-12 point): see Section 3.4 for discussion of the problems of exact definitions.

PATHOLOGICAL — diseased.

POINT SIZE (of type) — the printer's basic unit of measurement of type size, equal to 0·01383 inch or approx. 1/72 inch. Confusion can arise because in measuring type, it is the body size (i.e. the size of the metal on which the letter is cast) and not the size of the letter as printed, that is referred to. Thus the appearing size of a printed letter of the same point or body size can vary depending on the type face e.g. 12 point Times Roman

12 point Perpetua.

(see also X-HEIGHT)

PRESBYOPIA (presbyopic) — normal and gradual decrease in power of accommodation in the eye that starts in middle age.

READING TEST TYPES — charts used to test the visual acuity of the eye for close tasks like reading: see Appendix B.

RELIABILITY (of statistical results) — the extent to which a test is *consistent* in measuring what it does measure (cf. VALIDITY).

REPRODUCTION (method) — process by which multiple copies of a piece of printing are produced (and as distinct from the composition or type setting stage) e.g. letter-press, offset-lithography, electrostatic process.

RESIDUAL VISION — vision remaining in a pathological eye.

RETINA — the inner lining of the eyeball, containing the light receptors (rods and cones)

RETINAL DETACHMENT — the separation of the retina from the back of the eye which can lead to blindness.

RETINOPATHY — general term describing diseases of the retina occurring in cases of high blood pressure, renal deficiency and diabetes: loss of visual acuity is caused by retinal haemorrhages.

RETROLENTAL FIBROPLASIA — disease causing formation of a membrane behind the lens and resulting from excess of oxygen at birth of premature babies (now rare).

SERIF – the terminal stroke finishing off certain main strokes of a type face e. g. a serif type face.

SANS-SERIF (type face) – a type face without serif e. g. a sans serif type face.

SNELLEN CHART – standard sight testing chart used for clinical measurement of visual acuity: see Appendix B.

STATISTICAL SIGNIFICANCE – measure of the extent to which experimental results are due to chance. Conventionally accepted levels of significance for experimental results are:

* = "significant" = 5% level of significance = P (probability) < 0·05, meaning that there is less than 1 chance in 20 of observing such results if no real effects are operating

** = "highly significant" = 1% level of significance = P < 0·01, less than 1 chance in 100

*** = "very highly significant" = 0·1% of significance = P < 0·001, less than 1 chance in 1000

TYPE FACE – the style or design of a set of alphabetic or numeric characters: may include variations of the basic design to be used in combination e.g. medium, **bold**, *italic*. The names of type faces mentioned in this report include Plantin, Gill Sans, Century School Book, Caslon, Garamond, Imprint and Baskerville.

UNCORRECTABLE VISION – vision which is pathological and which is still defective even after refractive errors have been corrected by spectacles. (see also CORRECTED VISION)

UPPER CASE – capital letters e. g. A B C.

VALIDITY (of statistical results) – the extent to which a test *actually* measures what it is intended to measure (cf. RELIABILITY).

VISUAL ACUITY – the sharpness or clearness of vision: the power of the eye to distinguish form as opposed to colour.

WEIGHT or BOLDNESS (of type) – the degree of heaviness of a type face e. g. light, medium, **bold**: not to be confused with the colour or quantity of ink used for printing the type.

X-HEIGHT – the height of a lower case x: this varies between type faces of the same point or body size e.g. Times Roman has a large x-height and short ascenders and descenders. Perpetua has a small x-height and long ascenders and descenders. (see also POINT SIZE)

References

AMERICAN FOUNDATION FOR THE
BLIND
1968

Proceedings of the Research Conference on Geriatric
Blindness and Severe Visual Impairment, Sept. 1967

New York: American Foundation for the Blind

BABLOLA, J.
1961

The Facilitation of Reading by Partially Blinded
Persons.

Brit. J. Physiol. Optics, **18,** 220-234

BENNETT, A.G.
1965

Ophthalmic Test Types

Brit. J. Physiol. Optics, **22,** 238-271

BIRCH, J.W.,
TISDALL, W.J.,
PEABODY, R. &
STERRETT, R.
1966

School Achievement and Effect of Type Size on
Reading in Visually Handicapped Children

Co-operative Research Project No. 1766
Pittsburg: University of Pittsburg

BOARD OF EDUCATION
1934

Report of the Committee of Inquiry into Problems
relating to Partially Sighted Children (Crowley Report)

London: HMSO

BURT, C.
1960

The Readability of Type

New Scientist, **7,** 277-279

CARMICHAEL, L. &
DEARBORN, W.F.
1948

Reading and Visual Fatigue

London: Harrap

COHN, H.L.
1886

Hygiene of the Eye in Schools (trans. W.P. Turnbull)

London: Simpkin & Marshall

DEPARTMENT OF EDUCATION
& SCIENCE.
1968

Blind and Partially-Sighted Children

Education Survey No. 4.
London: HMSO

EAKIN, W.M.,
PRATT, J.A. &
McFARLAND, T.L.
1961

Type Size Research for the Partially Seeing Child

Pittsburg: Stanwix House

EDUCATION ACT 1944   London: HMSO
1944

FORTNER, E.N.   Investigation of Large Type Books
1943
          Proc. of 20th Biennial Convention of American
          Association of Workers for the Blind

GOLDSTEIN, H.   The Demography and Causes of Blindness
1968
          New York: American Foundation for the Blind

GOVERNMENT SOCIAL SURVEY   Mobility and Reading Habits of the Blind by
1968   P.G. Gray & J.E. Todd
          London: HMSO

HANDICAPPED PUPILS AND SCHOOL HEALTH SERVICE REGULATIONS: S.R. & O
1945   1945/1076
          London: HMSO

ILLUMINATING ENGINEERING   The IES Code: Recommendations for Good Interior
SOCIETY   Lighting
1961
          London: Illuminating Engineering Society

IRWIN, R.B.   Unpublished account of Large Type Reading Tests
          carried out in Conservation of Vision Classes in
          Cleveland, Ohio, 1919-20

KENDALL, M.G. &   Tables of Random Sampling Numbers
BABINGTON SMITH, B.
1960   *Tracts for Computers No. XXIV*
          Cambridge: University Press

KUNZ, J.E. &   Effect of Target Brightness on "Normal" and
SLEIGHT, R.B.   "Sub-normal" Visual Acuity
1949
          J. Appl. Psychol., 33, 83-91

LAW, F.W.   Reading Types
1952
          Brit. J. Ophthal., 36, 689-690

LICKLIDER, J.C.R.   A Crux in Scientific and Technical Communication
1966
          Amer. Psychologist, 21, 1044

LUCKEISH, M. &   Visibility: Its Measurement and Significance in
MOSS, F.K.   Seeing
1935
          J. Franklin Inst., 220, 431-466

MARKS, L.E. &   The Role of Semantic and Syntactic Constraints
MILLER, G.A.   in the Memorization of English Sentences
1964
          J. Verbal Learning & Verbal Behaviour, 3, 1-5

70

MEDICAL RESEARCH COUNCIL
1926

Report on the Legibility of Print by R.L. Pyke

London: HMSO

MINISTRY OF EDUCATION
1949

The Health of the School Child; Report of the Chief
Medical Officer for 1946 and 1947

London: HMSO

MINISTRY OF HEALTH
1955

Circular 4/55 National Assistance Act 1948,
Certification of Blindness and Partial Sight:
Form BD8

London: HMSO

MINISTRY OF HEALTH &
DEPT. OF HEALTH FOR
SCOTLAND
1959

Report of the Working Party on Social Workers in
Local Authority Health and Welfare Services
(Younghusband Report)

London: HMSO

MINISTRY OF HEALTH
1963

Circular 4/63 National Assistance Act 1948,
welfare services for the partially-sighted

London: HMSO

MINISTRY OF HEALTH
1966

The Incidence and Causes of Blindness in England and
Wales 1948-1962 by A Sorsby

Reports on Public Health and Medical Subjects No. 114
London: HMSO

MINISTRY OF HEALTH
1967

On the State of the Public Health; Annual Report
of the Chief Medical Officer for the year 1966

London: HMSO

MINISTRY OF HEALTH
1968

Annual Report for the year 1967

London: HMSO

MONOTYPE CORPORATION LIMITED
1966

Scientific Copyfitting

London: Monotype Corp. Ltd.

NATIONAL BUREAU OF
STANDARDS
1964 & 1967

Legibility of Alphanumeric Characters and
Other Symbols, I & II by D.Y. Cornog,
F.C. Rose & J.K. Walkowicz

Washington D.C.: U.S. Dept. of Commerce

NATIONAL SOCIETY FOR THE PREVENTION OF BLINDNESS, New York: written communication
September, 1967

NOLAN, C.Y.
1959

Readability of Large Types: a study of type sizes
and type styles

Int. J. Educ. Blind, 9, 41-44

1961 "

Legibility of ink and paper colour combinations for
readers of large type

Int. J. Educ. Blind, 10, 82-84

POULTON, E.C. &
FREEMAN, P.R.
1966

Unwanted Asymmetrical Transfer Effects with
Balanced Experimental Designs

Psychol. Bull. 66, 1-8

PRINCE, J.H.
1957

Relationships of reading types to uncorrectible lowered visual acuity

Amer. J. Optometry, 34, 581-595

1958 "

New reading material for sub-normal vision subjects

Amer. J. Optometry, 15, 629-636

1959 "

Special print for sub-normal vision patients

Amer. J. Optometry, 36, 659-663

1960 "

Visual acuity and reading in relation to letter and word design

Ohio State Univ. Inst. for Research in Vision Pub. No. 1

1966 "

Type for the Visually Handicapped (unpublished report to the American Library Association)

RAND, G.
1946

Relation between Illumination and Visual Efficiency

Arch. Ophthal., 35, 509-513

ROYAL NATIONAL INSTITUTE FOR THE BLIND

Unpublished account of studies carried out by the National Institute for the Blind in schools for the partially-sighted in the United Kingdom, 1928-38

SCHONELL, F.J.
1966

Graded Word Reading Test in *The Psychology and Teaching of Reading*

London: Oliver & Boyd

SCHONELL, F.J. &
SCHONELL, E.
1966

Basic Word List

London: Macmillan

SPENCER, H.
1969

The Visible Word

London: Lund Humphries

STEVENS, S.S.
1951

Mathematics, Measurement and Psychophysics in *Handbook of Experimental Psychology*

London: Chapman & Hall

TINKER, M.A.,
1963

Legibility of Print

Ames, Iowa: Univ. of Iowa Press

1965 "

Bases for Effective Reading

Minneapolis: Univ. of Minnesota Press

TREDREA, D.J.

Unpublished account of studies carried out in schools for the partially-sighted in the British Isles, 1964

WEALE, R.A.
1963

The Ageing Eye

London: H.K. Lewis

WEST, M.
1965

A General Service List of English Words

London: Longmans

WESTON, H.C.
1961

Rationally Recommended Illumination Levels
Trans. Illuminating Eng. Soc., 26, 1-16

WESTON, H.C.
1962

Sight, Light and Work
London: H.K. Lewis

WORLD HEALTH ORGANISATION
1966

Epidemiological & Vital Statistics Report:
Special Subject-Blindness 19(9)
Geneva: WHO

ZACHRISSON, B.
1965

Studies in the Legibility of Printed Text
Stockholm: Almqvist & Wiksell

Appendix A

Print Specimens (actual size)

The samples illustrated here are same-size reproductions of the printings tested. The variations in face, weight and spacing that were tested are shown in the 12 and 14 point sizes: the same variations were also tested in 16, 18, 20 and 24 point, but only single examples of these sizes are illustrated here. (For exact typographic specifications see table 6, p. 27). The 32 samples in 12 and 14 point illustrate the word content of the test passages.

```
Face:    GILL
Weight:  ROMAN
Size:    12 POINT
```

Main floors escape special loads. Foreign
glories arrange careful bills. Returning
fathers concern large merchants. Valuable
shadows know frequent corn. Lower money
beats straight diseases. Last oils enjoy

Spacing: "normal"

Wild life claims perfect witnesses. Loud
beauties move demanding chairs. Sad wages
attract silent populations. Exact spaces
please ideal dinners. Appointed plates see
lost farms. Deep newspapers expect square

Spacing: extra space
between letters
and words

Next season allows set companions. Modern
banks paint vain trade. Brave adventures
marry extreme churches. Ancient machinery
shoots future currents. Important stories
take late posts. Black clubs seize twenty

Spacing: extra space between
words only

Noble ways sing other bread. Long stores
perform second teeth. Religious fashions
compose wide factories. Excellent officials
appear usual towns. Sorry coals walk five
defences. Numerous flowers speak wrong

Spacing: extra space between
lines only

74

```
Face:    GILL
Weight:  ROMAN
Size:    14 POINT
```

Every advantage lays warm elections. Dear
notes aim observed thoughts. Grand visits
support various rates. Left journeys read
either thing. Managed steel believes sore
wives. Fancy productions account delivered

Spacing: "normal"

Public games hold all types. Real papers
admit offered losses. Dangerous citizens
build opposed necessities. Pure windows
receive probable stones. Distant memories
call this system. Low sizes catch pretty

Spacing:
extra space
between letters
and words

Shining lengths care his uncles. Circular
employers imagine entire neighbours. Two
pounds arrive full pictures. Open unions
have sweet parks. Angry silences reflect
cruel views. Cut appearances breathe wet

Spacing: extra space between
words only

Plain divisions keep worst ladies. Faint
books stretch near metals. Dry centuries
hang answering schools. Eaten presidents
stand firm knowledge. Iron yards lean rich
captains. Delightful reasons favour brown

Spacing: extra space between
lines only

```
Face:    PLANTIN
Weight:  ROMAN
Size:    12 POINT
```

Impossible salts prefer ready halls. Due
shoulders afford detailed friends. Sacred
doubts watch common nights. Pale grains
happen separate liberties. Royal husbands
carry ordinary colours. Kind scales draw

Spacing: "normal"

Yellow peace fills several rivers. Empty
places recognise copper mountains. Sure
experiences think acting passengers. True
coasts express small arguments. Northern
gases finish six castles. Female laws pay

Spacing: extra space between
letters and words

New plans get little programmes. Active
marriages hunt social bands. Red desires
rise content brains. Early abilities treat
well districts. Mere cities belong human
pressures. Faithful clouds accept better

Spacing: extra space between
words only

Recent tables buy friendly lakes. Strong
inches collect beautiful kingdoms. Whole
births suffer young birds. One habit adds
simple relations. Original troubles reply
proper sympathies. Another spot possesses

Spacing: extra space between
lines only

Face: PLANTIN
Weight: ROMAN
Size: 14 POINT

Eastern crosses organize weak costs. Slow
lists combine suggested balls. Cotton bays
touch used grass. Understood cars increase
commanding directions. Serious graves pull
generous origins. Strange evenings drink

Spacing: "normal"

Moral fights supply different points. Fat
sorrows break effective weights. Existing
fools save total ends. Likely facts look
pleasant standards. Far kings determine
capital judgments. Humble characters sell

Spacing:
extra space
between letters
and words

Old dates advance sick forests. Necessary
skies find artificial gifts. Sincere interests
show gay roads. National horses write dull
leaves. Hungry bridges describe expensive
farmers. Reduced minds remember merry

Spacing: extra space between
words only

Idle months prevent ripe heads. Wonderful
branches depend those senses. Favourite
circles try calm messages. Remaining sons
wear correct artists. Steady passages owe
driven governments. Seven corners follow

Spacing: extra space between
lines only

```
Face:   GILL
Weight: BOLD
Size:   12 POINT
```

Easy deeds press great letters. Western motions suppose famous tastes. Flat marks strike white languages. Heavy situations pass golden colonies. Permanent failures help much rain. Electric fortunes refuse

Spacing: "normal"

Bad pairs introduce local babies. Regular villages regard difficult accidents. Your camps pray most affairs. Personal summers feed popular gardens. Average waters love private centres. Sudden gates rule middle

Spacing:
extra space
between letters
and words

Fallen soils bend outside natives. Slight experiments pick cloth decisions. Peaceful milk hides same hospitals. Round plants join broad religions. Severe nations wish raw doctors. Peculiar scenes gain certain

Spacing: extra space between
words only

Declared positions shake able wheat. Past expenses attend first activities. General poets turn busy music. Eager crops apply chief ears. Particular armies forget only numbers. Terrible voyages decide medical

Spacing: extra space between
lines only

Face: GILL
Weight: BOLD
Size: 14 POINT

Our seas contain industrial laughs. Short eyes gather talking ruins. Natural boards run bitter manners. Figured businesses lie proud sands. Favourable girls become close families. Upper subjects discover earnest

Spacing: "normal"

Encouraged offices sound holy beds. More coins adopt secret fellows. Gentle forces send immense natures. Counted groups kill eight parties. Mechanical products teach single children. Dark sisters mention tall

Spacing:
extra space
between
letters
and words

Immediate songs wonder noticed fish. Safe hours rush these engineers. Chosen mines stay loyal committees. Violent education preserves few bodies. Steep races address back hearts. Such freedoms realise clever

Spacing: extra space
between
words only

Big terms destroy still poems. Cool wines refer opposite courts. Fourteen soldiers throw rapid crowds. Living oceans struggle flying glass. Soft departments work poor materials. Honest exercises hope feared

Spacing: extra space
between
lines only

```
Face:    PLANTIN
Weight:  BOLD
Size:    12 POINT
```

**Best virtues arrest fresh lights. Curious
gentlemen lead tender articles. Printed
fingers unite hot societies. Alive fields
cry sharp advice. Precious railways drop
liquid clothes. Double levels want solemn**

Spacing: "normal"

**Needed countries blow good agents. Rough
sugar continues nice quantities. Winning
customs develop grey fronts. Hard results
burn false amounts. Possible flags dare
alone matter. Dead values promise hollow**

Spacing:
extra space
between letters
and words

**Their opinions provide right towers. Nine
degrees protect quick judges. Equal ships
ride fine mornings. Narrow mothers sweep
free influences. Wise fruits spread thick
statements. Guilty classes remind patient**

Spacing: extra space between
words only

**Cheap battles intend fast animals. Scarce
presences base fair owners. Both actions
seem changed people. Wandering quarters
miss fierce connections. Green doors play
elder streets. Familiar movements settle**

Spacing: extra space between
lines only

Face: PLANTIN
Weight: BOLD
Size: 14 POINT

**Bright mills include smooth weather. Cold
daughters roll southern boxes. Rare events
means fired cases. Blue snows give moderate
canals. Successful victories bless lonely
inventions. Beginning health repeats fixed**

Spacing: "normal"

**Enough sleep reaches former air. Defended
walls live even questions. Limited pieces
remark bare youths. Clear wars heat thin
problems. Neither possession deals bottom
flames. Criminal bones prepare splendid**

Spacing:
extra space
between
letters
and words

**Armed examples lift musical seats. Grown
varieties attempt completed efforts. High
eggs fail many stars. That meat connects
fond voices. Practical faces divide least
women. Reasonable colleges employ stiff**

Spacing:
extra space
between
words only

**Aged enemies disappear rude queens. Some
officers enter spent noses. Trained causes
elect spare dogs. Wealthy sights put glad
brothers. Delicate chances explain alike
controls. Glorious masters study crowned**

Spacing:
extra space between
lines only

The experimental design used for the tests, (see Section 6·0), meant that each subject read only 4 out of the 32 possible typographic combinations. It was arranged that each subject read two passages in each face, weight and size, and one in each of the four spacings being tested. e.g. the printings below are the four printings read by one of the subjects.

Bad pairs introduce local babies. Regular villages regard difficult accidents. Your camps pray most affairs. Personal summers feed popular gardens. Average waters love private centres. Sudden gates rule middle

Face: GILL
Weight: BOLD
Space: 12 POINT
Spacing: extra space between letters and words

Old dates advance sick forests. Necessary skies find artificial gifts. Sincere interests show gay roads. National horses write dull leaves. Hungry bridges describe expensive farmers. Reduced minds remember merry

Face: PLANTIN
Weight: ROMAN
Size: 14 POINT
Spacing: extra space between words only

Cheap battles intend fast animals. Scarce presences base fair owners. Both actions seem changed people. Wandering quarters miss fierce connections. Green doors play elder streets. Familiar movements settle

Face: PLANTIN
Weight: BOLD
Size: 12 POINT
Spacing: extra space between lines only

Every advantage lays warm elections. Dear notes aim observed thoughts. Grand visits support various rates. Left journeys read either thing. Managed steel believes sore wives. Fancy productions account delivered

Face: GILL
Weight: ROMAN
Size: 14 POINT
Spacing: "normal"

Of the 32 test printings in 12 and 14 point, the *most legible* print was the specimen below:

Our seas contain industrial laughs. Short eyes gather talking ruins. Natural boards run bitter manners. Figured businesses lie proud sands. Favourable girls become close families. Upper subjects discover earnest

Face: GILL
Weight: BOLD
Size: 14 POINT
Spacing: "normal"

The *least legible* were the four below: there were little statistically differences between the four but some evidence that increasing space decreased legibility.

Face: PLANTIN
Weight: ROMAN
Size: 12 POINT

Impossible salts prefer ready halls. Due shoulders afford detailed friends. Sacred doubts watch common nights. Pale grains happen separate liberties. Royal husbands carry ordinary colours. Kind scales draw

Spacing: "normal"

New plans get little programmes. Active marriages hunt social bands. Red desires rise content brains. Early abilities treat well districts. Mere cities belong human pressures. Faithful clouds accept better

Spacing: extra space between words only

Recent tables buy friendly lakes. Strong inches collect beautiful kingdoms. Whole births suffer young birds. One habit adds simple relations. Original troubles reply proper sympathies. Another spot possesses

Spacing: extra space between lines only

Yellow peace fills several rivers. Empty places recognise copper mountains. Sure experiences think acting passengers. True coasts express small arguments. Northern gases finish six castles. Female laws pay

Spacing: extra space between letters and words

All the variations in face, weight and spacing reproduced in this appendix in 12 and 14 point, were also tested in 16, 18, 20 and 24 point: only single examples of these sizes are shown below.

16 POINT

Fallen soils bend outside natives. Slight experiments pick cloth decisions. Peaceful milk hides same hospitals. Round plants join broad religions. Severe nations wish raw doctors. Peculiar scenes gain certain

18 POINT

Eastern crosses organize weak costs. Slow lists combine suggested balls. Cotton bays touch used grass. Understood cars increase commanding directions. Serious graves pull generous origins. Strange evenings drink

20 POINT

Impossible salts prefer ready halls. Due shoulders afford detailed friends. Sacred doubts watch common nights. Pale grains happen separate liberties. Royal husbands carry ordinary colours. Kind scales draw

24 POINT

Big terms destroy still poems. Cool wines refer opposite courts. Fourteen soldiers throw rapid crowds. Living oceans struggle flying glass. Soft departments work poor materials. Honest exercises hope feared

Appendix B

Snellen Sight Screening Chart (reproduced here at approx. $\frac{1}{3}$ actual size), used at 6m. with spectacle correction

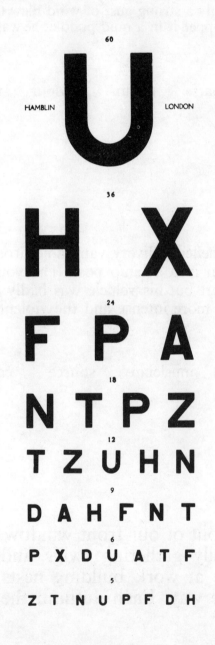

When I was walking through the woods I saw a bear standing on his hind legs. I ran to get my gun but when I returned it had gone. Suddenly a strong gust of wind blew the man's hat off his head and dropped it in a mud puddle: he was annoyed for it was

accuse   coarse   mourn   saviour   nonsense   income

12   12

The red-panelled delivery van came around the corner too fast and ran into a lamp post. The young driver was not seriously hurt but his vehicle was badly damaged. The rain storm grew more intense and the violent wind almost blew

announce   musician   source   career   numerous

14   14

Looking out of our front window I watched some birds busily gathering twigs and bits of straw: they were at work building nests in the treetops across the way. Each autumn the apple trees are

commence   excursion   nervous   minor

16   16

These last few days the weather has been hot and all of our milk has turned sour, so now we can hardly wait for the milkman

occasion   cease   enormous   assume

18   18

The muddy water sucked at the corners of the houses and swirled round the tree-trunks: everything disappeared in

serious   ancient   convince

20   20

Elephants drink water by filling their long trunks full and then squirting it into their mouths

rumour   insurance   camera

24   24

The present pub-
lication addresses
itself, in a popular
and inviting form,
to foreigners who
may wish to con-
vey to their res-
pective countries
correct ideas of
London.

N.48.

Modern Lon-
don, 1805.

**Sight Screening Chart (actual size), used at 35cms.
with spectacle correction**

REDUCED SNELLEN DISTANCE TYPES

Equivalent at 14 inches to

N	6/60
T P	6/36
X U Z	6/24
A Z F D	6/18
H T A P U	6/12
D X A Z U F	6/9
P H F B U T X	6/6

2	6/60
0 5	6/36
3 6 4	6/24
4 9 5 2	6/18
6 0 4 9 3	6/12
5 8 3 2 0 6	6/9
. . . .	6/6

Library Association Research Project
SCREENING CHART

89

Appendix C

Interview Questionnaire

LIBRARY ASSOCIATION
READING MATERIAL FOR THE PARTIALLY SIGHTED   Subject No.............
Experimental Series 1

Subject No		Test No		Vision						

Test Order	Sentence Content						Typography			Rel. Size	Read. dist-ance	Read. Time (secs.)	No. of errors	Rank Order
	12/14	14/16	16/18	18/20	20/24		Face	Weight	Space					
1														
2														
3														
4														

Interviewer's Comments

1	Date of Interview	2 Place of interview	1/2
3	Illumination		3
4	Name	5 Sex N/F	4/5
6	Are you going to use spectacles for these reading tests	Yes/No	6
7	" " " " " a magnifying glass " "	Yes/No	7
8	" " " " " low vision aids " "	Yes/No	8
9	Vision Screening: L.A. Chart at 35 cms (both eyes)		9
10	Reduced Snellen at 35 cms		10
11	L.A. Chart at own distance "		11
12	Chosen distance		12
13	Snellen distance chart at 6 metres - left eye		13
14	" " " " " - right eye		14
15	" " " " " - both eyes		15
16	Age last birthday 21 - 25 36 - 40 51 - 55 66 - 70 81 - 85		16
	26 - 30 41 - 45 56 - 60 71 - 75 86 - 90		
	31 - 35 46 - 50 61 - 65 76 - 80 over 90		
17	Where have you lived most of your life	Town/Country	17
18	What sort of work did your father do		18
19	Age when you left school/college		19
20	What was your first job when you left school		20
21	Marital status	N/S/W/D	21
22	What sort of work does/did your husband do		22

23	Are you working now	Yes/No	23
24	What was your last/present job		24
25	Have you ever had to change your job because of eye trouble	Yes/No	25
26	If YES to 25: How old were you when this first happened		26
27	Have you ever worn spectacles OR I see you wear spectacles	Yes/No	27
28	If YES to 27: How old were you when you first had them		28
29	When do you wear them now don't/always/close work/distance		29
30	When did you last have them checked ago		30
31	Have you ever used a magnifying glass or low visual aid	Yes/No/Given it up	31
32	If YES to 31: What for /reading/crosswords/sewing/knitting/at work		32
	Now I would like to ask you some questions about what you do in your spare time		
33	Do you watch T.V.	Yes/hardly ever	33
34	If YES to 33: How often almost every day/occasionally		34
35	If hardly ever or occasionally: Why not no set/eyestrain/no interest		35
36	Do you go to the theatre or cinema now	Yes/No	36
37	If YES to 36: How often regularly/occasionally		37
38	If NO or occasionally: Why not can't afford it/eyestrain/no interest		38
39	What other things do you enjoy doing now:		39
	check list Making things/sewing/knitting/mending		
	Painting and drawing		
	Reading music		
	Collecting things		
	Card games/chess/crosswords		
	Gardening		
	Radio		
40	Can you still do your own housework/shopping/cooking	Yes/No	40
41	Have you had to give up anything because of your eyes	Yes/No	41
42	If YES to 41: What		42
43	You have/haven't mentioned reading: Do you read much /Yes/No/a little		43
44	Have you ever borrowed books from a library regularly/occasionally/No		44
45	Do you borrow books from a library now Yes/Given it up		45
46	What are you able to read now:		46
	check list Newspaper headlines		
	Newspaper and magazine articles		
	Books		
	Ulverscroft/NLB Series		
	Books on tape		
47	What did you enjoy reading when your eyes were stronger?:		47
	check list Newspapers - which		
	Magazines - "		
	Books - romances history		
	mysteries biography		
	westerns funny books		
	war stories travel		
	Have you a favourite author..................................		
	Did you have to read much at work..................................		
48	Registration	Blind/Partially Sighted	48
49	Clinical Information		49

Analysis Coding Sheet

Library Association
Reading Material for the Partially Sighted - PUNCH CARD CODING

Item No.		Item No.	Col. Nos.
1	Subject No.	1	1-3
2	Test No.	2	4-6
3	Test Size	3	7-8
4	Sentence Content - Test 1	4	9-10
5	Face and Weight	5	11
6	Space	6	12
7	Rel. Size	7	13
8	Reading Time	8	14-17
9	Correct words	9	18-19
10	Sentence Content - Test 2	10	20-21
11	Face and Weight	11	22
12	Space	12	23
13	Rel. Size	13	24
14	Reading Time	14	25-28
15	Correct words	15	29-30
16	Sentence Content - Test 3	16	31-32
17	Face and Weight	17	33
18	Space	18	34
19	Rel. Size	19	35
20	Reading Time	20	36-39
21	Correct words	21	40-41
22	Sentence Content - Test 4	22	42-43
23	Face and Weight	23	44
24	Space	24	45
25	Rel. Size	25	46
26	Reading Time	26	47-50
27	Correct words	27	51-52
28	Chosen Reading Distance	28	53-54
29	Preference	29	55-56
30	Sex	30	57
31	Use of specs, mag. or l.v.a. for reading tests	31	58
32	Vision Screening - L.A. chart at 35 cms.	32	59
33	Reduced Snellen at 35 cms	33	60
34	L.A. chart at own distance	34	61
35	Distance Vision Screening	35	62
36	Age last birthday	36	63-64
37	Socio-Economic class	37	65
38	Education	38	66
39	Duration, severity and effect of defect	39	67
40	Use of optical aids at present time	40	68
41	Use of eyes at present time	41	69
42	Interest in reading	42	70
43	Use of library	43	71
44	Print reading at present time	44	72
45	Reading tests	45	73
46	Registration	46	74
47	Clinical information	47	75-80

Index by P.W. Plumb

(Topics which are clearly identifiable from the Contents are not indexed)

22472